ENDORSEMENTS

Dr. Curran takes you around the world to introduce you to a new dimension of prayer, then provides the tools to bring them home to your own prayer life. This book on prayer is an apostolic revelation for the closing hours of this dispensation. Sue penned the words, but it is clear that the Holy Spirit gave the utterance.

—John Kilpatrick

Dr. Curran's experiential grounding of this vital spiritual requirement provides the inspiration and motivation to all who want to develop or enhance their prayer life. I encourage every serious student of the faith to make this book a biblical companion and benefit from its wisdom and revelatory insights.

—Dr. Myles Munroe
Bahamas Faith Ministries International
Nassau, Bahamas

Prayer in the Another Dimension provides the missing link between the timid, reserved prayer posture of the American church and the bold, fervent, and persistent prayers of Christians in many other nations. Within the pages of this book lie the secrets that will take the prayer life of any individual, church, or citywide prayer network to a new level of releasing God's Kingdom in the earth today. If you've been looking for a prayer life that produces extraordinary results, you'll find the answers you've been seeking in Sue Curran's practical and inspirational new book.

—Cheryl Sacks
BridgeBuilders International
Phoenix, Arizona

As a general, Dr. Sue Curran sounds an alarm that praying in another dimension is the last move that shall precede the coming of the Messiah.

—Archbishop Nicholas Duncan-Williams
Christian Action Faith Ministries Worldwide

PRAYER IN ANOTHER
DIMENSION

PRAYER IN ANOTHER DIMENSION

Discover the Keys to the Next Level of Prayer

SUE CURRAN

DESTINY IMAGE® PUBLISHERS, INC.

P.O. Box 310, Shippensburg, PA 17257-0310

"Speaking to the Purposes of God for this Generation and for the Generations to Come."

This book and all other Destiny Image, Revival Press, Mercy Place, Fresh Bread, Destiny Image Fiction, and Treasure House books are available at Christian bookstores and distributors worldwide.

For a U.S. bookstore nearest you, call
1-800-722-6774.

For more information on foreign distributors, call
717-532-3040.

Or reach us on the Internet:
www.destinyimage.com

ISBN 10: 0-7684-2506-9

ISBN 13: 978-0-7684-2506-2

For Worldwide Distribution, Printed in the U.S.A.

1 2 3 4 5 6 7 8 9 10 11 / 09 08 07

TABLE OF CONTENTS

FOREWORD

This classic is truly a masterpiece for our generation. As a general, Dr. Sue Curran sounds an alarm that praying in another dimension is the last move that shall precede the coming of the Messiah. God is calling the Church to this dimension of prayer, which is designed to release the end-time harvest and launch the Church into a realm of unspeakable glory and supernatural activities before the Second Coming of the Lord. This book is pregnant with revelatory insights and strategic information that will unleash a hunger and passion for new dimensions of prayer.

In Psalm 141:2, David said, "Let my prayer be set before You as incense, the lifting up of my hands as the evening sacrifice." Thus we see that David likens the burning of incense with the offering of prayer. In ancient Israel the altar of incense had horns, which are symbolic of the power of prayer. There was one horn on each corner, which suggests that this power is equally available to all people and equally effective in all parts of the world. The testimonies chronicled in this book do justice to the power of prayer around the world and give preeminence to God's authority and activities in the earth.

I highly recommend this book for all who are truly seeking to ignite the flames of divine fire in their spirit, churches, communities, and around the world.

—Archbishop Nicholas Duncan-Williams

INTRODUCTION

Would you like to pray prayers that really get answers? Do you desire to touch the supernatural power of God in prayer? Do you wonder why you hear of mighty miracles and revival in other nations, but do not see them in your life? In your church?

You may be weary of hearing about revival fires and phenomenal church growth in other nations. Not weary of their good news, of course, but aching with longing to tap into this supernatural power yourself, that you might experience these wonders in your life, your church, your community. If so, I have good news for you. You can experience the same supernatural power of God as these other nations are experiencing. You simply have to learn to draw from the same source that is empowering them.

I have been privileged to be involved in revival moves throughout my years in ministry. It was during the Charismatic Renewal of the early 1970s that the church my husband, John, and I founded was birthed. Then, a sovereign prayer revival in our church in 1980 became the turning point in my life and ministry. Our church experienced the presence and power of God in awesome intensity as He moved mightily in our midst for three months, night and day. Our three daily prayer services often became one all-day meeting, as we waited in His presence continually, watching Him transform lives through deep conviction and repentance. During the months and years that followed, God's manifest presence empowered and enlarged our ministry, giving us national and international impact in the harvest.

Another powerful move of the Spirit, beginning in 1994, brought our church into a fresh experience of the tangible power and presence of God. There were unusual manifestations accompanied by physical and emotional healing and deliverance. As I traveled in ministry, this wonderful presence of God was manifest wherever I went, with awesome results of changed lives.

More recently, I began to encounter ministries in other nations that were continually empowered in this spiritual realm, yet with greater results. They were seeing miracles of healing and deliverance that were rarely seen in the American church. In every situation, I traced the source of their empowerment to a *lifestyle of prayer* that was different from our Western idea of prayer. I soon realized that it wasn't just different; it was a greater, more powerful dimension of prayer.

Through traveling to participate in Prayer Summits and networking with many of the spiritual leaders of these "revival" nations, I have embraced the principles of the kind of praying that breaks the chains of darkness, sickness, and demonic power. I am sharing in this book, not just better methods of prayer, but revelatory insights and strategies that can elevate you to a completely new dimension of prayer. From experiences shared in this book, you will learn, among other things:

- The power of vocal prayer.

- The need for fervent prayer.

- The principle of praying the Word of God.

- The freedom to focus on God alone.

- The authority of prophetic declarations.

Churches in nations such as Korea and China have discovered and embraced a powerful mentality toward prayer, different from our Western mind-set. Nations in Africa and South America are being transformed by the power of God through this lifestyle of prayer. As you read this book, you will explore the differences and learn to put into practice the same prayer dynamics that have made our brothers and sisters in these nations effective in the harvest. In addition, you will be empowered to pray in that spiritual realm that is designed to release the Church in our nation into the next great move of the Spirit of God. I invite you to join me in my journey to *prayer in another dimension.*

CHAPTER 1

A SUPERNATURAL POWER SHIFT

Revival Fires Burning

There is a well-known expression that says: "One half of the world doesn't know how the other half lives." Though this often applies to the disparity of living conditions and economic privilege, it is also proving to be true concerning the work of God in the earth today. I do not believe that Christians determine to be uninformed or ignorant of God's power that is being manifest in many nations of the earth. Yet, there is a powerful, miraculous moving of God's Spirit in "one half" of the world today, which has gone largely unnoticed by "the other half." This phenomenal revival happening in Asia, Africa, China, and South America is not a recent one, but one that has been increasing for several decades, bringing in a harvest of millions of souls.

Western Christians, who were once the great force in world missions, are now outnumbered four-to-one by non-Western

Christians. During the 1980s, Christianity was growing world-wide at a rate of 2 percent a year; now it is growing at a rate of 8 percent annually, fueled by revival fires burning brightly in developing nations. Islam, which is growing at a rate of 2 per-cent annually, has taken a backseat to this phenomenal growth of Christianity in other nations.

People desperately need the supernatural power of God to resolve their dilemmas.

In America, there has been a mega-shift from growth in tra-ditional denominational churches to the "new apostolic church movement" of interdenominational, charismatic churches. Even the liberal-biased news media has focused on the phe-nomenal growth of this movement in our nation. These are churches that establish the truth of the supernatural power of God manifested through the working of the gifts of the Holy Spirit. Miracles of healing, deliverance from drug addiction, healed marriages, and transformed lives are giving witness to the power of God at work in these believers' lives. While denominational churches continue to decline in membership in our nation, these churches are growing at a rapid rate.

People desperately need the supernatural power of God to resolve their dilemmas. When they see convincing proof of the power of God transforming lives around them, they are drawn to God's presence. I am convinced that by focusing on what God is doing supernaturally in the earth today, we can take hope that He will send a mighty revival to our nation.

The fact that we see God saving souls en masse and performing signs and wonders in other nations of the earth indicates that there is a good chance He will do the same in greater measure in our nation than we are presently seeing. The revival many American Christians long for may be closer than we think. If we can learn to "get God's attention" as these believers in other nations have obviously done, we can be a part of bringing revival to our desperately needy nation.

THE BURDEN OF THE LORD

As the author of *Prayer in Another Dimension*, I feel it is incumbent upon me to explain to the reader why it was important to write yet another book on the topic of prayer. I want to articulate the primary purpose for its message. Along with explaining the purpose of this book, let me also relate to you the *burden* of my message. I believe this book is the result of a God-given mandate to share hope with disheartened, disappointed Christians, who are stuck in a religious paradigm and mired in frustrated dreams. There is hope for those believers who are not content to have "church as usual," where they attend for one hour a week and then go out to face the challenges of life feeling unprepared to do so. And there is hope for the frantically active, overworked Christians who are disillusioned by the lack of success they are having in bringing in a harvest of souls.

"God is no respecter of persons" (Acts 10:34 KJV).

The purpose of this book is to show you how to cooperate with God's plan to manifest His supernatural power and presence in your life, in your family, in your church and your community. For all believers who are longing to see the power of God made manifest in the church, whatever denominational "label" you wear, I have a burden to share with you the good news—God wants to answer your cry. God desires to make His Kingdom a reality in the earth; He desires to fulfill the promises of His Word in your life and in the life of your church.

In short, God desires to do in the American church the same wonders of salvation, healing, and deliverance that He is manifesting in many other nations of the earth at the present time. It is a biblical principle that "God is no respecter of persons" (Acts 10:34 KJV); He desires to reveal His love and power to all people everywhere. We must recognize, however, that there are prerequisites—conditions—for seeing the power of God manifested in a life, a church, a nation. One of those conditions is set forth clearly in the Word of God:

> *...if My people who are called by My name will humble themselves, and pray and seek My face, and turn from their wicked ways, then I will hear from heaven, and will forgive their sin and heal their land* (2 Chronicles 7:14).

The purpose of this book is to motivate, inspire, and instruct Christians to seek God in a more powerful dimension of prayer. This prayer in another dimension, which believers in other nations are experiencing, is breaking the chains of voodoo and occult power, and resulting in unusual miracles— even raising the dead. And they are reaping a mighty harvest of souls unlike any we have seen in our lifetime. Their megachurches are not program based, not even "small group" based. These churches are founded on and empowered by the biblical pattern of prayer and personal evangelism that we read of in the Book of Acts.

As Christians who are undoubtedly living in the last days, we must not settle for living a comfortable life and doing the best we can in an ungodly world. We dare not be content with enjoying the peace of God for ourselves and seeking personal blessing. We must connect with the heart of our Savior, who came to "seek and to save that which was lost" (Luke 19:10). In order to experience the victory of Calvary in our personal lives and to be a part of bringing in the harvest, we must learn to activate our faith in the ways we see Christians in other nations doing. Then we can expect God to do His wonders among us.

Among the things you will learn as you read this book are:

1. The power of vocal prayer.

2. The need for fervent prayer.

3. The principle of praying the Word of God.

4. The "vertical" perspective—focusing on God alone.

5. The authority of prophetic declarations.

---

*You will be inspired to personal victory
and to fulfill the Great Commission.*

As you read this book, I believe you will be inspired to personal victory and to fulfill the Great Commission. You will also receive "tools" to help you succeed in fulfilling your destiny in God. Putting into practice the principles discussed here will empower you to live in victory and to reap a harvest of souls. As we discuss keys that our brothers and sisters in Africa, China, and other nations are using effectively to bring in the harvest, I pray that revelation will come to your heart to be able to do the same. And as we explore the hindrances to our praying fervently in another dimension, I believe the Holy Spirit will convict and cleanse your heart, so that you can be among those used effectively by God to bring a great end-time revival to our nation.

ANOTHER DIMENSION FOR OUR "PRAYING CHURCH"

It has been almost 20 years since I wrote my book, *The Praying Church*,[1] which describes the powerful prayer revival we experienced at Shekinah Ministries, the church my husband, John, and I founded in 1973. The book, which was birthed out of our experience of God's manifest presence through corporate prayer in 1980, gives practical instruction in forming and maintaining corporate prayer meetings for churches. It is not based on theory, but on what we learned from the sovereign move of God in our midst. Translated into several languages, it is used as a textbook by many pastors and churches, with wonderful results. Peter Wagner calls it "simply the best book on the subject."[2]

I am grateful for how God has used that book. But the main reason I mention it is simply to state that though we are not strangers to the powerful move of God through prayer, we have recently been introduced to another dimension of prayer. We have experienced its power as we have worked with ministers from other nations where God is pouring out His Spirit.

In 1974, at the beginning of our work, the Lord had inspired us to take a real step of faith in launching the ministry to which we were called, though we still had little idea of what our God-given mission was. We simply wanted to raise up a body of believers in our area who desired the full gospel message and we sought to instruct believers to live the "Sermon on the Mount." From the very beginning, prayer was not just an option for us. We had taken such a step of faith, in relation to the size of our small congregation, that we *had* to pray to move forward into God's purposes. We purchased 160 acres near the interstate, which God showed us was the place He had ordained for this ministry.

We built our sanctuary and other facilities with our hands during the day and prayed together every evening. Those were years of incredible labor, real sacrifice, and unforgettable joy, as we cast ourselves on God and His promises. In the past 30 years, we have built a beautiful conference center and developed a supportive congregation to facilitate our international headquarters for leadership training. Besides the local church ministries, we have established a conference ministry, foreign missions outreaches, and an Antioch Fellowship of ministers. The effectiveness of corporate prayer has been the key to success for every aspect of this ministry.

---

*I sensed a real need for our people
to be established in a lifestyle of fervent prayer.*

Having left our Methodist "roots" after receiving the baptism of the Holy Spirit, we began to pray fervently for the purposes of God to be accomplished in our lives. We saw the power of God provide all we needed in miraculous ways to establish the ministry that God was giving us. This supernatural provision was awesome to us, unlike anything we had experienced before. As the work continued to grow, we learned that our prayer lives also had to grow in measure with His blessing. Even in those early years, I sensed a real need for our people to be established in a *lifestyle* of prayer.

As I taught the congregation concerning prayer, I encouraged everyone to give at least one hour a day to the Lord in private prayer. I taught that it was best to set aside an hour in the morning for prayer, to allow them to seek God for His will for the day ahead. As a result, they became established in a personal devotional life. The church leadership prayed together often as well. And I personally have cultivated a lifetime habit of spending the first half of each morning in prayer.

Our hearts were hungry for revival. In 1979, for a full year, I taught the whole church on biblical principles of prayer during a Saturday evening service. Then we would divide into small groups to pray. As we look back to those days of "learning," we have to admit that some of those prayer meetings were a trial! But we had to start somewhere. We wanted to know the power of God in revival, which we had read about in the Scriptures and in church history. We did not want to have church "as usual," which we had despaired of in our denominational churches. And we learned many lessons about how to develop an effective prayer life, even through trial and error, discarding methods that didn't "work."

Suddenly...

Then, suddenly, one Sunday morning in late February of 1980, we experienced a powerful move of the Holy Spirit in our church service. The convicting presence of the Spirit of God gripped our hearts. We set aside the following week to pray, planning to meet together morning, afternoon, and evening for prayer. As we began that week of prayer, the Lord came to us again in such power that the morning prayer meeting ran into the afternoon prayer meeting, which ran into the evening meeting!

God melted our hearts in worship before Him. He brought us to deep repentance and wonderful cleansing. He gave new songs of abandoned worship, which became revival songs for the congregation. He gave fresh revelation of His Word and filled us with deep longings to know Him and to seek His presence. And He infused our hearts with faith for the ministry outreaches He had ordained for us.

---

*The convicting presence
of the Spirit of God gripped our hearts.*

During the years that followed, God brought people from many nations of the earth to our Bible Institute and allowed us to teach them the truths we had learned of prayer, worship, and revival. These students later established wonderful ministries in India, Germany, Indonesia, South Africa, and other nations. The Holy Spirit also directed us to host worship conferences, establish a Christian academy, develop missions outreaches in many nations, publish books, and begin ministry outreaches in our community.

The Holy Spirit remained with us in this powerful intensity of day and night corporate prayer meetings for three months, and the saturation presence of the spirit of prayer continued in strength for an entire year. Experiencing that life-changing season in the manifest presence of the Lord brought our congregation into a realm of prayer that the devil has never been able to rob from our church. God established us during that time as a *house of prayer*. Though we would be personally involved in many facets of international ministry, we understood that our primary purpose was to be a house of prayer. It was Jesus who declared: "Is it not written, 'My house shall be called a house of prayer for all nations'?" (Mark 11:17). In our zeal to build a place where the commandments of Jesus could be lived, the Holy Spirit taught us that the central purpose for the Body of Christ is to be a people of prayer. Based on that understanding, we have continued to develop a lifestyle of prayer for the past 25 years.

Seeking for More...

We have established morning prayer meetings two days a week for those who are available to pray. We also pray together as a congregation every Saturday night, to prepare the atmosphere for the moving of the Holy Spirit in the Sunday services. Each church service begins with 20 minutes of united prayer as a congregation. We also intercede for the lost and seek the purposes of God for our individual lives and ministry as we pray corporately.

Small prayer groups meet during the week for special "assignments" in prayer as well. We host prayer retreats to teach foundational principles of prayer and to pray believers into new realms of victory. In addition, we have a prayer chain that is notified of special needs and crises that need immediate attention. We are developing prayer teams, healing teams, and deliverance teams to minister to the specific needs of the Body of Christ and the community as well. As a result of learning to be a house of prayer, a many-faceted ministry has developed, taking us to the nations. We have networked with hundreds of ministers in this nation for fellowship, training, and encouragement as well.

We are seeking God
for greater empowerment in prayer.

It is against this backdrop of a prayer lifestyle that we are seeking God for greater empowerment in prayer—*in another dimension*—not from a prayerless posture, but from one of diligence to an established lifestyle of prayer. It is our relationship with ministers and spiritual leaders of other nations that has allowed us to witness a greater realm of the supernatural power of God as we observe their lives and ministries. We are seeking greater power, faith, and understanding of the kind of prayer they are involved in that is reaping a tremendous harvest of souls.

What do these Christians from other nations have to teach us that will make a difference in our godless culture, which has turned to hedonism and atheistic philosophies at an alarming rate? How can entire nations in Africa now be called "Christian," when they once worshiped at the shrines of voodoo and witchcraft? Is their conversion simply because of God's sovereign choice, or do believers have a part to play in God's moving in the earth? It seems that they do. Our cry is to know the "God of the African," and of other nations that are experiencing God's transforming power through prayer. We want to learn God's ways so that our nation can be impacted as these nations are with the message of salvation, healing, and deliverance.

ENDNOTES

1. Sue Curran, *The Praying Church* (Lake Mary, FL: Creation House Press, 2001).
2. Ibid., Peter Wagner cover endorsement.

CHAPTER 2

A CRY FOR AMERICA

Where Is the Revival?

You may be aware that current statistics report a lack of growth in the American church, which seems especially dismal for us when we look at the phenomenal growth of churches in many nations of Asia, Africa, South America, and even the former Soviet Union. Kevin Turner, director of Strategic World Impact in Bartlesville, Oklahoma, is an evangelist who ministers primarily in regions of the world where the gospel is restricted. He comments on the state of the American church in general:

> We have large buildings and many programs but still no move of God. We have more trained ministers and more Bible colleges than any other nation but no revival. We have seminars on revivals and huge campaigns to promote our meetings. But where is the revival? We have spotless theology but no doxology—we have no song in our hearts.[1]

Turner continues his observations regarding the cause of our spiritual downfall:

> We have replaced true experience with hyperactivity.…
> As a church we are power-hungry and covet top positions as if we are climbing a corporate ladder.… We forget that spiritual authority is not given to the savvy businessman or the sports hero but to those who have carried the burden of the Lord. Where are the brokenhearted believers who weep through the night over our spiritual bankruptcy?[2]

THE PRIORITY OF PRAYER

Contrast this grim but sad reality of the state of the American church with the apostolic ministry of Natalia Schedrivaya, who is involved in training an army of peasant Christians to plant 300 churches in unreached areas of Siberia. They are not wealthy, and are persecuted by communists as well as by Russian Orthodox priests, yet they are traveling from village to village to share the gospel.[3] They live their lives denying the natural human tendencies to seek first of all our personal comfort, well-being, and safety, as well as our own pleasures. Such commitment, zeal, and sacrificial living to propagate the gospel at the risk of their lives is the result of supernatural empowerment through prayer.

Joseph D'souza, president of the All India Christian Council and associate international executive of OM International, a global missionary agency, works among the Dalit people, a marginalized group in North India. Dalits are viewed by other

Indians as "untouchables." In recent years, hundreds of thousands of Dalits have come to Christ. D'souza says they record a new case of persecution against Christians at least every 36 hours. Like India, the people of Sudan, the Middle East, and China know great sorrow. However, Christians in these countries also know great joy as they see God moving with supernatural power that triumphs over the worst persecution.[4]

Rather than allowing this news of God's manifest power working in other nations to discourage us, let me say that I believe this powerful move of God is the best news we have heard in years. I believe it should encourage Christians everywhere to cry out to God to do for our nation what He is doing for others. Archbishop Nicholas Duncan-Williams, one of my African mentors, declared, "In the Old Testament, Daniel found out how to 'get God's attention' concerning Israel, through fasting and prayer, crying out to Him."[5] "Getting God's attention" requires obedience to His Word and following the biblical pattern of prayer, which these spiritual leaders of other nations are doing effectively.

Where God Is Moving

For the past 30 years the spiritual power center has been shifting from the Western nations to nations we consider "developing nations." There has been a huge growth in numbers of converts to Christianity in these nations, while in nations like America, churches are stagnant or declining. Even American churches that boast an increase in numbers are woefully lacking in the miraculous, supernatural power of God. In other nations, there are numerous reports of miracles such as physical healings. It is reported that there are documented cases of people being raised from the dead in 52 countries![6]

Although the focus of this book is not on miracles, I mention them to draw your attention to the fact that the supernatural power of God is moving in the earth. While God's power is not moving overwhelmingly in Western nations, powerful revival fires are burning in other nations. Our culture has known great awakenings and mighty revivals in the past. Entire denominations were spawned as a result and thousands of missionaries were sent to the corners of the earth. However, today, Western nations are not experiencing the power of God at present as these other cultures are enjoying. I do not believe this is because God has abandoned Western nations, but because Western nations have abandoned God. These developing nations have discovered the secrets to releasing the supernatural power of God through abandoning themselves to *prayer in another dimension.*

Natalia Schedrivaya states bluntly:

Materialism is the No. 1 enemy of Russian churches in the big cities, just as it is in the United States. Today pastors are not praying about how to reach those who have not heard the gospel. They are praying, "God, how can I have a megachurch?" Persecution has played an important role in church growth in Russia. Most of the miracles that took place in our villages happened as a result of God turning severe persecution and resistance into victories.[7]

Persecution of "Affluence"

So, should we pray for persecution in order to see the power of God? Hardly. Persecution is not a biblical prerequisite for revival. Yet, in a very real sense, we endure our own cultural form of persecution caused by our *affluence*, which distorts our priorities, jades our values, and confuses our goals. Any force that militates against the believer's pursuit of God can be considered persecution, whether that be government policy or personal greed. Still, we must recognize the deception for what it is or we will continue to live the "status quo" established in our churches and religious lives.

Key to winning souls:
the power of consistent corporate prayer.

For example, is it more important to you to see the power of God redeem your children from this corrupt generation, or to work long hours to provide for them the latest electronic gadget they want? Do you seek God diligently in prayer to save the lost, or do you put in more hours to perfect the latest church program that will draw them in? Are you content to enjoy temporal comforts of home, car, bank account, retirement, and vacations, or do you have a sincere desire to win the lost to Christ? Too often, apathy and complacency are the result of financial prosperity that nurtures a politely religious self-centeredness. To the extent that prosperity militates against hunger for God and His presence, it is by definition an insidious form of "persecution."

Natalia Schedrivaya concludes:

I am not against prosperity. I am happy to enjoy God's material blessings. And I am happy to see megachurches as long as they are involved in making disciples.... Yet I live in a country where you have to trust God for the smallest things: to buy food, get on the bus or find a doctor. The revival taking place today is in Russian villages (not in the cities), where God is raising an army of peasant Christians who have been equipped to win souls. These missionaries, evangelists, pastors and apostles are not wealthy, and they are persecuted by communists as well as by Russian Orthodox priests. Yet they are traveling from village to village to share the gospel. To me this is church growth.... Practicing the presence of Jesus daily is the key.[8]

"Practicing the presence of Jesus daily is the key."
—Natalia Schedrivaya

The fact is that other nations have been experiencing for many years the miraculous power of God for tremendous ingathering of souls as well as healing and deliverance. And this revival movement has been sustained and continues to expand because of its *priority of prayer*. Not based on successful programs or proper publicity, their churches thrive based solely on the central focus of prayer.

Dr. David (Paul) Yonggi Cho, founded his church, Yoido Full Gospel Central Church of Seoul, Korea, 50 years ago. Today, the church has more than 850,000 members. It was one of the first of megachurches to call attention to the key to winning souls: *the power of consistent corporate prayer*. Yet, many American pastors who visited Dr. Yonggi Cho's church and endeavored to "transplant" this Korean church's early morning and all night prayer meetings to their American churches failed. Their sad testimony is that, generally, they achieved little success in sustaining such intense corporate prayer in their churches.

Apathy and Complacency

There simply was not the desire, hunger, or fortitude in American churches to seek God like their brothers and sisters in Korea were willing to do. These pastors had observed the zeal and commitment to prayer in the Korean church, but were unable to transfer its reality to their American congregations, which were filled with apathy and complacency. Pastors consistently tell me, "We can't get our people to pray" or "We don't have zeal about prayer."

American churches have largely forsaken the lifestyle commitment to prayer that we see in other nations. Many of our churches have undergone great changes in the last few years to try to accommodate our Western lifestyles. Acknowledging the need for change in the face of dwindling church membership and attendance, church leaders have responded by trying to accommodate the *preferences* of their members. So they restyled their music, their dress code, their "image." However, none of these socially acceptable accommodations increase the supernatural power level of the church or make it more effective in winning souls. We need to receive a greater revelation of the dynamic at work in the prayer-centered churches of other nations in order to begin to see the Kingdom of God manifested in power in our nation.

As individuals, as well as churches, we like to make changes that allow us to feel "current" and "in the know." The changes we resist are the ones that require a paradigm shift. However, when we acknowledge the truth that what we are doing and the way we are doing it is not *working*, we must become willing for radical change.

Sadly, there is often not even the expectation that the church will have a vital prayer ministry. In other words, churches are being built on the wrong foundation. According to Jesus' own declaration, a church is to be a "house of prayer" (Mark 11:17). It is time to seek for a true spiritual change in our nation's churches—a dramatic paradigm shift that will deliver us from church tradition and allow us to become new wineskins.

ENDNOTES

1. Kevin Turner, "Why Isn't the American Church Growing?" *Charisma* (Lake Mary, FL: Strang Communications, January 2005).

2. Ibid.

3. Ibid., Natalia Schedrivaya.

4. Ibid., Joseph D'souza.

5. Archbishop Nicholas Duncan-Williams, Senior Pastor, Action Worship Center, 9759 Mountain Laurel Way, #1B, Laurel, MD 20723; www.actionworshipcenter.org, author of *Binding the Strong Man*, *Praying Through the Promises of God*, and other titles.

6. James Rutz, *Megashift: Igniting Spiritual Power* (Colorado Springs, CO: Empowerment Press, 2005), p. 30.

7. Kevin Turner, "Why Isn't the American Church Growing?" *Charisma* (Lake Mary, FL: Strang Communications, January 2005).

8. Ibid., Natalia Schedrivaya.

CHAPTER 3

THE OTHER HALF OF THE WORLD

Keys to Revival

For more than four years after the intensity of our prayer revival at Shekinah had subsided, we were still walking in a powerful corporate prayer lifestyle. Such was the grace of God on our lives, that though many of us work together in close proximity in our many-faceted ministry, I did not personally hear a word of "backbiting" among the congregation during those years. Our outreaches have continued to expand, new doors for mission involvement have opened, and other facets of leadership training have been established as a result of the powerful lifestyle of prayer that was established during that awesome outpouring of the Spirit in our midst.

That prayer revival taught us how to maintain an effective corporate expression of prayer as a congregation, which I document in my book, *The Praying Church*. Among the wonderful results of that revival is the fact that it enlarged our spiritual capacity to hear and receive the Word of God; it filled us with desire to know His miraculous working in our midst on an ongoing basis. As a result, our hunger for the power and presence of God has led us to continually investigate His phenomenal moving—wherever we hear it happening. My personal search for the "heart" of revival has led me to investigate this powerful prayer movement in many nations.

As I have ministered in "the other half of the world," in nations that are enjoying the supernatural move of God, I have looked for the keys to their prayer ministry. In Bogotá, Colombia, I preached in a church of 30,000 pastored by Enrique Gomez, a converted warlock. Their sanctuary, a former warehouse in downtown Bogotá, seated 10,000 at the time. They are continually purchasing property in the adjacent red-light district, as they reap a harvest of street people and prostitutes through the power of corporate prayer. Their radio station, named appropriately, "Cadena de Amor" (Chain of Love), beams across the entire area, declaring the love of Jesus to all who will hear. Their people enter the sanctuary to pray and are "interrupted" only for the praise service and a message from the Word of God. Pastor Gomez teaches a simple message to his people: "Receive Christ, fast and pray, and then go tell others about His great love."

Another church where I witnessed a phenomenal dimension of prayer is El Shaddai Church in Guatemala City, Guatemala, pastored by Harold Caballeros. They have a prayer meeting they call "Seven Hours of Power," during which the entire congregation focuses on praying fervently until the power of God is released into their midst. They are witnessing a wonderful harvest of souls and are taking back the territory that once belonged to satan.

I also observed a tremendous prayer outpouring of an entire congregation during the crusade ministry of Carlos Annacondia, when I visited with him in Mar del Plata, Argentina. He stations 200 intercessors under the makeshift platform for his open-air crusades; these believers pray continually while he preaches and ministers healing and deliverance to the multitudes. Another ministry team prays for the deliverance of people, including children and youth, who have become steeped in witchcraft and all manner of occult practices. Even witches themselves attend and are delivered from the power of satan to serve Jesus Christ.

Annacondia, a successful businessman, is not an ordained minister. He is simply a compassionate man who is successfully running his own factory while preaching the gospel to the poorest of the poor and training teams to pray for those who are bound by the devil. He avoids using stadiums for his meetings—though he has been invited to because of the mighty miracles occurring in his ministry—because he wants to reach the people who could not or would not attend. Through his ministry, several million converts have come to Christ since the 1980s. Carlos Annacondia is credited with bringing a sweeping revival to his country, and surrounding countries as well, through the power of God released as people abandon themselves to *another dimension of prayer*.

More recently, in my search for keys to greater power in prayer, my path has sovereignly led me to some outstanding leaders from Africa. Archbishop Nicholas Duncan-Williams is known as the father of the Charismatic movement in Ghana.[1] He is recognized by his president and high government officials, who request his prayer and his presence during personal and national crises. Over the past 20 years he has raised up a church of about 15,000 in the city of Accra. Like Yonggi Cho and others, he has done it through the supernatural power of prayer that has triumphed over dark, demonic powers, which threatened to kill him.

The son of a wizard, Duncan-Williams has, of necessity, invoked the supernatural power of God, in his sheer struggle for survival, to overcome the powers of darkness that wanted to destroy his life. His personal need to defeat the reality of demonic power entrenched in his ancestors and his nation has driven him to experience the supernatural reality of *prayer in another dimension*. He is now sharing keys to unlocking the power of God with churches in many nations, with similar supernatural results.

The prayer power of these African leaders involves a dimension of divine revelation beyond what we have known generally in our American churches. This kind of prayer is powerful and effective in "destroying the works of the evil one" (see 1 John 3:8). For these leaders and their churches, prayer is a way of life—not an occasional experience. They pray with authority that releases the Spirit of God to perform salvation, healing, miracles of finances, breaking of curses, and setting people free to fulfill their destiny in God. They rebuke the cosmic elements to avert destruction from storms; they uncover the plots of the devil against individual lives, gaining the victory over his destructive purposes before the believer can be harmed.

Prayer is a way of life—not an occasional experience.

As I have studied their written materials and been mentored personally by these powerful African leaders, I have ministered this fresh revelation of prayer in another dimension to my congregation. Even though we had embraced the lifestyle of a "praying church," it took about a year for us to grasp this fresh revelation and make the transition into this new dimension of prayer.

During that time, we also received the ministry of several of these powerful African ministers from Ghana, Nigeria, and other nations. And I traveled to Ghana to experience a large prayer summit among Archbishop Duncan-William's churches. We also hosted prayer summits at our church, where African leaders ministered to us and to which we invited other churches and ministers with whom we are networked. The power of God was released in a fresh way upon many lives, and many testified to the fire of God ignited in their hearts. Miracles of healing as well as financial breakthroughs and other mighty victories have resulted from the powerful prayer we experienced during these summits.

A Paradigm Shift

The principles of prayer God taught us in our prayer revival are necessary and viable for the foundational prayer life of every believer. We cannot expect to enter another dimension of power in prayer without walking faithfully in these foundational principles. Yet, we are learning from our African brothers and sisters the keys to expressing greater authority and faith in prayer. We are receiving fresh fire and empowerment to abandon ourselves to prayer as never before. I was amazed that the Holy Spirit used one clear, powerful statement to help me make the transition from our foundational models of prayer to introduce me to a greater dimension of prayer. That statement came from a sermon by Nicholas Duncan-Williams. He exhorted us simply: "Stop this Western praying."

"Stop this Western praying!"—Duncan-Williams

I knew that the prayer principles God had taught us in our prayer revival did not represent "Western praying." They were valid foundational truths regarding prayer. Yet, we were definitely seeing greater power, miracles, and harvest in the lives and ministries of these African leaders. So I listened, as he continued: "These nice prayers are not going to get you anywhere. You've got to get mad at the devil."

Greater Revelation

I understood that the "Western praying" to which Duncan-Williams referred is an insipid, faithless, lacking-in-authority-and-focus prayer, which is characteristic even of many sincere believers. Though in our experience we had established a solid foundation of prayer principles, we were being introduced to a new level of authority, focus, and greater revelation of the supernatural power of prayer that brings greater biblical results.

This new dimension of prayer teaches us to focus on recognizing the defeat of the devil (which Christ accomplished on the cross) and to insist on his immediate release of every good thing that God has promised to His children. These African leaders understand the divine imperative of wrestling "*against principalities, against powers, against the rulers of the darkness of this age, against spiritual hosts of wickedness in the heavenly places*" (Eph. 6:12). They have learned to contend for the promises of

God to His children in order to live the abundant life—in every area of life.

In addition, they have genuinely, and of necessity, embraced the authority that Jesus gave to His disciples: *"All authority has been given to Me in heaven and on earth. Go therefore and make disciples of all the nations, baptizing them in the name of the Father and of the Son and of the Holy Spirit"* (Matt. 28:18-19). Living focused lives as the Scriptures teach, and spending much time in the Word and in prayer, these beautiful, radical Christians have released the power of God in the earth to such an extent that they are seeing their entire nations coming to Christ.

In our American church, I taught and modeled, in a deliberate and determined way, this powerful revelation we were receiving of prayer in another dimension. Yet, our congregation struggled to experience this new dimension of prayer, which required a greater level of faith. We needed a paradigm shift to break through into this spiritual realm. Even as a praying congregation, we had to be willing to break down past "religious" traditions and mentalities that limited our power in prayer. We had to establish the biblical framework for a new level of supernatural empowerment in prayer. This level of prayer involves hand-to-hand combat with the unseen forces arrayed against us. It requires a willingness to do spiritual warfare against the principalities and powers of the devil.

Prayer Is Many-Faceted

Of course, prayer is many-faceted and involves the entire worship life of a believer and a congregation. The apostle Paul admonished believers to put on the whole armor of God to be able to stand against the devil's schemes. Then he instructed them to *"pray in the Spirit on all occasions with all kinds of prayers and requests"* (Eph. 6:18 NIV).

We cannot live without prayers of repentance, petition, praise, and thanksgiving. The precious times of worship that we seek, when we spend time in communion with Jesus, are vital to our spiritual life. This new dimension of prayer that we are seeking involves every facet of prayer. Fuchsia Pickett, who was a mentor to me, describes the seven "moods" of the Holy Spirit in prayer as "convicting, counseling, compassionate, cleansing, commanding, and conquering."[2] Learning to yield to the Holy Spirit's moods in prayer requires much time spent in His presence, consistently, in what I have called a *lifestyle of prayer.*

Focus on recognizing the defeat of the devil!

It is a divine principle that every facet of prayer must be breathed upon by faith and the power of the Holy Spirit. Whether we are rebuking the devil in hand-to-hand combat or praising the goodness of our God, we are dependent on the Holy Spirit. He alone can increase our faith and empower us to pray more effectively and with greater results.

If we are to experience in our nation the revival for which many of us long, we will have to embrace the foundational biblical principles of corporate prayer. We will also need to open our hearts to receive further revelation of the level of faith and power in prayer that is being so powerfully manifested today in other nations.

SEEING THROUGH THEIR EYES

It is common knowledge that prayerlessness has become an epidemic in American churches. I applaud *Charisma* magazine for their recent article addressing the needs of the American church, as seen through the eyes of leaders from other nations where God is moving in revival. In the article they interviewed leaders of the megachurches in other nations, asking them for their observations (not criticisms) of the American church. Almost with one voice they concluded that the ills of the American church can be traced to the fact that they have left the place of prayer.[3]

In addition to the problem of prayerlessness in the American church, they also observed: (1) a lack of pursuing a holy lifestyle, (2) people ruling rather than the pastor, (3) program-oriented organizations rather than a presence-oriented organism, (4) low obedience level, and (5) a lack of commitment to making disciples.[4]

"There is a price to pay for revival."
—Enoch Adeboye.

To understand the powerful impact that these large churches in Ukraine, Korea, Africa, and other nations are having on their once godless nations, our focus needs to be on the *kind* of praying that has resulted in producing their national impact. What have they learned about prayer that has empowered them to establish praying churches in this dimension of power? Obviously, they have learned what authority in prayer really is and what it does, and they've learned how to sustain the fervency of it on a corporate level. They have debunked traditional, religious mentalities and approaches that have drained the life and spiritual reality of prayer from so many of our churches.

If you could get a million people to attend a monthly meeting called simply "the Holy Ghost Meeting," where people would come to pray, to listen to prophetic exhortations, and to witness miracles, you would be considered a "powerful leader in the faith." Other Christian leaders and believers would consider it valuable to know what you know. Enoch Adeboye of Nigeria is such a spiritual leader. General Overseer of the Redeemed Christian Church of God, one of the fastest growing churches in the world, he is establishing churches in many parts of the world. Consider his evaluation of the keys to revival:

> There is a price to pay for revival. It takes a lot of sacrifice. A revival takes us back to the basics of Christian principles that are fast disappearing from the Christian horizon. This includes a disciplined life of sincere holiness and a life devoted to prayer and frequent fasting.[5]

I believe we are on the threshold of a fresh move of God's Spirit in America. When God is getting ready to move He instills a hunger in those who desire to be involved in what He is presently doing in the earth. As we continue to explore the keys to effective prayer that is bringing the fire of God to many parts of the world, I encourage you to open your heart to receive new revelation from God. As you become willing to commit your life to effective prayer, God will hear your cry and empower you by His Spirit.

ENDNOTES

1. Archbishop Nicholas Duncan-Williams, www.actionworshipcenter.org.

2. Fuchsia Pickett, *Presenting the Holy Spirit: Who Is He?* (Lake Mary, FL: Charisma House, 1997).

3. Kevin Turner, "Why Isn't the American Church Growing?" *Charisma* (Lake Mary, FL: Strang Communications, January 2005).

4. Ibid.

5. Ibid., Enoch Adeboye.

CHAPTER 4

THE FOURTH DIMENSION

The Spiritual Realm

Even now, in our nation, there are prayer organizations dedicated to bringing believers together to cry out to God for revival for our nation. Cheryl Sacks, director of The National Church Prayer Leaders Network, has written a book entitled *The Prayer Saturated Church*,[1] which is aimed at helping local churches become a house of prayer. Pastor C. Peter Wagner and Chuck Pierce have established the United States Strategic Prayer Network. And Pastor Dutch Sheets of Springs Harvest Fellowship has traveled with Chuck Pierce to all 50 states, gathering groups of praying people to seek God's direction in prayer for their states.[2] Mike and Cindy Jacobs are cofounders of Generals International, a ministry committed to seeing nations transformed through intercessory prayer.[3]

These are just of a few of the godly men and women God is raising up to bring transformation to our nation through prayer.

In addition, our nation is blessed at present with a president who prays daily and takes every opportunity to call our nation to prayer.

However, our churches are not overwhelmingly character- ized by a deep dedication to a *committed lifestyle of prayer*. Too many Christians (and even pastors) in our American churches consider prayer an "option," seeking supernatural intervention only when our own resourceful initiatives don't seem to be working. Others relegate intense, fervent prayer to those with the "gift" of intercession. Sadly, there are even large churches that have not been built on the biblical foundation of prayer. These churches are merely religious and social organizations, offering something for everyone. They have not touched the reality that churches are established to serve the will of God in the power of the Holy Spirit—through effective prayer.

---

*These churches are merely
religious and social organizations.*

A Chinese Christian recently visited the United States and toured many churches here. At the end of the trip he was asked what he thought about American spirituality. He answered, "I am amazed at how much the church in America can accom- plish without the Holy Spirit."[4] He saw large, beautiful sanctuar- ies, elaborate programs for every age, and plentiful social activities, but did not sense the presence and power of the Holy Spirit working among the people.

While we can establish organized congregations and reli- gious activities, we cannot expect to have the presence of God without prayer. We cannot know His power and His miracles without fervent, faith-filled praying—in another dimension. The loss of these spiritual realities is a tremendous price to pay for the *privilege* of prayerlessness.

American Intellectualism

Americans are not given to understanding spiritual realities, either of the Kingdom of God or the kingdom of satan. Our culture has embraced science and the intellect, through which we interpret all "reality." Yet, the denial of the spiritual realm has created a terrible void in the lives of millions of people because we are created as spiritual beings. It is into this "spiritual" void that the occult world is making inroads in people's minds through psychics, mediums, horoscopes, Ouija boards, tarot cards, palm reading, games like Dungeons and Dragons, and yes, even *Harry Potter*.

The denial of the spiritual realm has created a terrible void.

As a result, many children and youth, along with adults, are becoming more curious about the supernatural world of the occult, in the absence of foundational biblical teaching about the supernatural realm of the Kingdom of God. In these and other ways, the devil is creating destructive bondages in the minds and hearts of millions of people. The devil, whose goal is to "steal, kill, and destroy" (see John 10:10), is filling unsuspecting minds with desires for suicide and other deadly means for self-destruction. Only the truth of the gospel can set them free from the many deceptions of the evil one.

Jesus gave us the answer to overcoming this evil "strong-man": *"But when a stronger than he comes upon him and over-comes him, he takes from him all his armor in which he trusted, and divides his spoils"* (Luke 11:22). Only as we connect with the "stronger" power of God through prayer can we be empow-ered to overcome the evil of the strongman, who uses his power to deceive and blind men and women to the wonderful love of God.

Dr. Cho's Transformation

In 1979, Dr. Yonggi Cho wrote a book entitled *The Fourth Dimension.*[5] I remember reading it soon after it was published. But as I have reread it more recently, the book has impacted me in a different way. Earlier I made mention of the fact that Dr. Cho is among those who built his church on the bedrock of prayer as a *lifestyle.* Karen Hurston is the daughter of John Hurston, who was the sole partner with Yonggi Cho in the early days of establishing the great Yoido Full Gospel Church. I have received a good understanding of the inner dynamic of his min-istry through conversations with my friend Karen. She related to me that Dr. Cho attributes the transformation of his life and ministry to his discovery of the truth of the fourth dimension— *the spiritual realm.*

We can only learn to pray in another dimension when we receive the revelation that there is another dimension—that it exists as an eternal reality. Let's consider for a moment the meaning of the term "dimension." Simply put, a *line* exists as a one-dimensional reality; a plane represents a second dimension, and a *cube* the third dimension. The first dimension, a line, is contained in, and therefore controlled by, the second dimension, a *plane*; this second dimension is included in, and therefore controlled by, the third dimension, the *cube*. The material world and the whole earth belong to the third dimension.[6]

> *Our human race is much more than*
> *a three-dimensional entity.*

Our own bodies are a wonderful three-dimensional reality, a marvel of our benevolent Creator. Yet our human race is much more than a three-dimensional entity, contrary to what atheists purport. The Creator of all things brings us to the fourth dimension of which all mankind is a part—*the spiritual realm*. Transcending the other three dimensions of the material world, the Creator exists in the fourth dimension of the spirit world: "God is Spirit" (John 4:24). He is controlling the other three dimensions by virtue of His having made them. He created mankind in His own image, which makes us spiritual beings.

In the Genesis account of creation, the Scriptures declare that the Spirit of God hovered over the dark, formless void of the earth. Then, as God spoke, He created every form of life as we know it, bringing order out of the chaos of the earth. When God created man, He said, "Let Us make man in Our image, according to Our likeness. ...So God created man in His own image; in the image of God He created him; male and female He created them" (Gen. 1:26-27). Because the Scriptures also declare that God is Spirit, we must conclude that mankind, made in the image of God, is not a mere physical being, relating only to the third dimension. We were created in the image of

God, who is Spirit, and are meant to relate to the fourth dimension as spiritual beings.

The fourth dimension involves a spiritual realm that is without substance and is undetectable for the most part by our senses or our intellect. Yet it is the most powerful realm of reality that exists. The spiritual realm relates to God the Father, God the Son, and God the Holy Spirit. Unfortunately, it also relates to the realm of evil spirits and to satan himself, a created spiritual being that rebelled against God and has warred against His purposes in the earth since before time began (see Isa. 14).

Your human spirit dwells in the realm of the fourth dimension. God warned Adam and Eve that if they disobeyed His command not to eat of the tree of the knowledge of good and evil, they would surely die. When Adam and Eve disobeyed God, the death they experienced was first of all spiritual—they became alienated to their eternal relationship with God. Oswald Chambers explains the nature of this spiritual death:

> Soul and body depend upon each other, spirit does not—spirit is immortal. Soul is simply the spirit expressing itself in the body...Spirit has never died, can never die, in the sense in which the body dies; the spirit is immortal, either in immortal life or in immortal death. There is no such thing as annihilation taught in the Bible. The separation of spirit from body and soul is temporary. The resurrection is the resurrection of the body.[7]

Adam and Eve became candidates for immortal death because of their disobedience to God and, as a result, caused the entire human race to be born into a sinful state, alienated in our spirit from God. Ultimately, they died a physical death as well, which was never God's plan. In order to become alive again to God, Jesus taught plainly, "Unless one is born again, he cannot see the kingdom of God. ...Unless one is born of water and the Spirit, he cannot enter the kingdom of God" (John 3:3,5).

We can only learn to pray in another dimension when we receive the revelation that it exists.

A vital, living relationship with God, who is Spirit, is only possible to those who are born again of the Spirit by accepting Christ as Savior. He died a terrible death on the cross in order to reconcile to God the entire human race, every person who would accept the sacrifice of Christ's blood for our sin. The heart of God is the heart of a heavenly Father, seeking to establish relationship with sons and daughters who seek to worship Him "in spirit and truth" (John 4:23). When we are born again, the Spirit of God indwells our spirit, making possible again our communication and communion with Him. According to the Scriptures, we are saved by grace through faith: "For by grace you have been saved through faith, and that not of yourselves; it is the gift of God" (Eph. 2:8). Titus explains clearly:

But when the kindness and the love of God our Savior toward man appeared, not by works of righteousness which we have done, but according to His mercy He saved us, through the washing of regeneration and renewing of the Holy Spirit, whom He poured out on us abundantly through Jesus Christ our Savior, that having been justified by His grace we should become heirs according to the hope of eternal life (Titus 3:4-7).

Believers have been born again by the wonderful grace of God, through faith, which is God's gift to us. So the realm of the spirit—the fourth dimension—is a realm of faith expressed through our human spirit. Dr. Paul Yonggi Cho explains:

You are not a common creature (just another animal), for you have the fourth dimension in your heart, and it is the fourth dimension that has dominion over the three material dimensions—the cubical world, the world of the plane, and the world of the line. Through dominion in the fourth dimension, the realm of faith, you can give order to your circumstances and situations, give beauty to the ugly and chaotic, and healing to the hurt and suffering.[8]

It is the plan of God for the fourth dimension to rule over the third dimension—the spiritual world to rule the material world. He desires for His Kingdom of "righteousness and peace and joy in the Holy Spirit" (Rom. 14:17) to be manifest on this earth. It is in the fourth dimension that either good or evil is created. For example, evil was introduced into the human race when Eve saw (imagined) that the fruit of the forbidden tree was "good for food, that it was pleasant to the eyes, and a tree desirable to make one wise" (Gen. 3:6). In her imagination, she toyed with the idea of eating the fruit, allowing her spirit to be enticed by the idea of becoming as wise as God. She was spiritually deceived, and when she gave the fruit to her husband, they both lost their innocence before God. They were cut off from their spiritual communion with God. And in their alienation from God, the entire human race became alienated from Him.

Christ died to establish our relationship with God again, making it possible for the good of the spiritual world to be manifest in our lives. Unfortunately, millions of people have been introduced to the evil of the fourth dimension through occult practices. Entire cultures have been terrorized by witch doctors who demonstrate the dark powers of the devil. These evil spiritual realities, existing apart from God, are totally destructive. Even in our nation, the occult has been given a "legitimate" status as a religion, which is taught in many of our high schools. We dare not negate the reality of this evil, which has the power to destroy lives.

Godly spiritual life, quickened by faith in God, creates order and beauty. It answers the prayer Jesus gave us to pray: "Thy kingdom come, Thy will be done in earth, as it is in heaven" (Matt. 6:10 KJV). As we unite our minds—our visions and dreams—with the purposes of God, we are empowered to create the beautiful spiritual Kingdom of God on the earth. For this reason, the Scriptures are filled with instructions regarding our thoughts such as: "Let this mind be in you which was also in Christ Jesus" (Phil. 2:5), and "...be transformed by the renewing of your mind, that you may prove what is that good and acceptable and perfect will of God" (Rom. 12:2).

When we heal the sick or raise the dead we are to declare, "The kingdom has come near you." The Kingdom of God emanates from the realm of the Spirit, which is a realm of faith—the fourth dimension. As born-again believers, by releasing our faith in prayer, we can bring the manifestation of the Kingdom of God to earth. (Of course, when Jesus returns He will establish His physical kingdom in the earth.) The apostle

Paul declared that we are living temples of God (see 1 Cor. 3:16), and that "we have this treasure in earthen vessels" (2 Cor. 4:7). The life of God dwelling in our spirit wants to manifest the love of God to the world.

---

*It is the plan of God for the fourth dimension
to rule over the third dimension.*

LAWS OF THE FOURTH DIMENSION

The laws of the godly spiritual world are different from the laws of the natural material world. For example, when describing the Kingdom of God, Jesus taught unusual things like, "In My Kingdom, he who wants to be great among you must be the servant of all" (see Matt. 20:26-27). And He insisted that it was right to "love your enemies" and "bless those who curse you" (Matt. 5:44). We call these "kingdom principles." It is obvious that these principles do not belong to the world; unbelievers (and even some Christians) demonstrate the opposite of these godly characteristics, seeking to be served and inventing ways to "do their enemies in." The Kingdom of God belongs to the fourth dimension and is to be manifested in the life of the born-again believer.

The laws of the evil fourth dimension—the spiritual realm of the devil—war against the purposes of God in the earth. Jesus stated this fact simply, contrasting His Kingdom with the devil's: "The thief does not come except to steal, and to kill, and to destroy. I have come that they may have life, and that they may have it more abundantly" (John 10:10). Jesus cast out many unclean or evil spirits that tormented people and gave authority to His disciples to do the same (see Mark 16).

Prayer Causes War in the Heavenlies

The Scriptures indicate that there is a hierarchy of evil spirits that war against God's purposes. Jesus referred to the *"prince of this world"* (John 12:31 KJV), stating that he will be "cast out." The apostle Paul states clearly that all unbelievers are under the control of this evil prince. Writing to believers, he declares:

> *And you He made alive, who were dead in trespasses and sins, in which you once walked according to the course of this world, according to the **prince of the power of the air**, the spirit who now works in the sons of disobedience, among whom also we all once conducted ourselves in the lusts of our flesh, fulfilling the desires of the flesh and of the mind, and were by nature children of wrath, just as the others* (Ephesians 2:1-3).

Evil spirits war against God's purposes.

According to the Scriptures, there are powerful named princes that rule over nations and regions of the earth. For example, the angel told Daniel that he had been hindered from bringing the answer to his prayer by the "prince of the kingdom of Persia" (Dan. 10:13). The angel had to fight with the same evil spiritual ruler on his return (see Dan. 10:20). This evil prince obviously had authority over a nation and determined what would pass through his domain. God's response to Daniel's prayer required war in the heavenly realm between angelic beings and an evil prince of satan's kingdom. Those evil forces ruling Persia were conquered by angelic forces, *in response to Daniel's prayer.*

Binding the Strongman

We mentioned that Jesus taught the principle of binding the strongman before we are able to spoil his goods. He said:

> *But if I cast out demons by the Spirit of God, surely the kingdom of God has come upon you. Or how can one enter a strong man's house and plunder his goods, unless he first binds the strong man? And then he will plunder his house* (Matthew 12:28-29).

It is a biblical principle that the strongman is an evil master spirit set over a life, a city, a region, or an entire nation. There can be a strongman set over a church whose purpose is to keep it from growing and thriving. These evil spirits work diligently to keep people from gathering to an established local church and to scatter those who do. They work through the self-life of believers to create dissension, conflict, and division (see James 4). Until the strongman is bound and cast out through fervent prayer, God's purposes for His Church cannot be realized. Satan wants to abort the divine assignment each of us has to deliver the captives who are bound in darkness.

Breaking Strongholds

Jesus declared, "When a strong man, fully armed, guards his own palace, his goods are in peace" (Luke 11:21). In other words, the strongman creates a fortress or "stronghold" that keeps his "goods" from suffering any harm. The strongman is satan and his "goods" are the souls of men. He creates strongholds in their minds that blind them to the truth. He binds them, making them slaves of sin, wrong thinking, bad habits, and destructive relationships. He blinds their minds to keep them from coming to salvation and enjoying the freedom that Jesus alone can give.

Often, territorial spirits are responsible for a mind-set for an entire region or culture. They may convince people that religion is a "crutch" for the weak, or that the homosexual lifestyle is normal, or even that God is dead. Religious spirits rule entire organizations through false doctrines and cultish practices. False religions are also satanic strongholds that rule entire nations. The apostle Paul understood the spiritual battle involved in pulling down strongholds and setting these captives free when he wrote:

> For though we walk in the flesh, we do not war according to the flesh. For the weapons of our warfare are not carnal but mighty in God for pulling down strongholds, casting down arguments and every high thing that exalts itself against the knowledge of God, bringing every thought into captivity to the obedience of Christ, and being ready to punish all disobedience when your obedience is fulfilled (2 Corinthians 10:3-6).

The apostle Paul also acknowledges that satan hindered him on more than one occasion from getting to where he wanted to go. He wrote to the church at Thessalonica, "We wanted to come to you—even I, Paul, time and again—but satan hindered us" (1 Thess. 2:18). When we become convinced that "we do not wrestle against flesh and blood, but against principalities, against powers, against the rulers of the darkness of this age, against spiritual hosts of wickedness in the heavenly places" (Eph. 6:12), then we will begin to walk in the victory of the fourth dimension. The apostle Paul describes the armor of God necessary to our victory, including "praying always with all prayer and supplication in the Spirit" (Eph. 6:18).

As I have experienced the power of prayer in this fourth dimension, I have preached concerning the wonderful life-changing influence it gives to every believer. If you would like to study more on the subject, I encourage you to order my *Fourth Dimension* audio series from our online bookstore.[9]

Religious spirits rule entire organizations.

ENDNOTES

1. Cheryl Sacks, *The Prayer Saturated Church* (Colorado Springs, CO: Pray! Books, NavPress, 2004).

2. Chuck Pierce, "Prayer News Alert": pna@strategicprayer.net.

3. Cindy and Mike Jacobs, cofounders, Generals International: http://www.generals.org/.

4. Kevin Turner, "Why Isn't the American Church Growing?" *Charisma* (Lake Mary, FL: Strang Communications, January 2005).

5. Dr. David Yonggi Cho, *The Fourth Dimension* (Gainesville, FL: Bridge-Logos, 1979).

6. Ibid., pp. 38-39.

7. Oswald Chambers, *Biblical Psychology*, as quoted in *My Utmost Devotional Bible*, (Nashville, TN: Thomas Nelson Publishers, 1992), p. 1038.

8. Dr. David Yonggi Cho, *The Fourth Dimension* (Gainesville, FL: Bridge-Logos, 1979), p. 66.

9. Sue Curran, *Fourth Dimension Audio Series*, 4 tapes for $15.00. Please order from our online bookstore at www.Shekinah.net.

CHAPTER 5

EMBRACING SPIRITUAL REALITIES

A Paradigm Shift

Twenty years ago, when Dr. David (Paul) Yonggi Cho wrote his extraordinary book, *The Fourth Dimension*, he was reluctant to present the message to Western readers because he did not feel they were ready to receive it. He understood the intellectual and scientific approach to life that most Western nations have adopted, which denies the reality of the spiritual realm. Even Christians have often negated the truth of the supernatural realm, which is manifest in the lives of believers in Korea and other nations as the powerful reality of prayer and faith.

It is not that we are incapable or that people in these other nations are "better" than us. It is a mind-set—our mentality— that inhibits us. We have read the Scriptures in the light of our scientific and intellectual paradigm, which has distorted our theology and severely limited our experiencing the power of

God. Unwittingly, we have allowed the laws of the third dimension to dominate our spiritual lives, which are meant to be subject only to the law of faith in the fourth dimension. We have become spiritually bankrupt because we have embraced a faulty paradigm for evaluating the fourth dimension. To enter into the spiritual reality of God's revival power will require a paradigm shift for many believers.

God challenged the apostle Peter's religious paradigm, which he had received from his understanding of the Scriptures. He was challenged to violate his beliefs and embrace a way of life he had thought was contrary to the Scriptures. You may remember that he was praying on the rooftop when he received a vision from Heaven in which he was encouraged to eat the kinds of food the Scriptures taught were unclean. Peter knew the vision was from God, for he responded, "Not so, Lord! For I have never eaten anything common or unclean" (Acts 10:14).

God challenged the apostle Peter's
religious paradigm.

His immediate response to the vision was to reject it completely, based on his understanding of the law's requirements for righteousness. Yet, God was using this vision to introduce Peter to a larger spiritual dimension of His divine grace, which He intended to pour out on all Gentiles. The vision was not about food, essentially. It was about a religious paradigm in which Jews considered Gentiles to be unclean. Throughout the Old Testament Scriptures we read that Israel was instructed not to mix with Gentile nations. Even Jesus sent His disciples out, saying, "Do not go into the way of the Gentiles, and do not enter a city of the Samaritans. But go rather to the lost sheep of the house of Israel" (Matt. 10:5-6).

Now it was time to fulfill Old Testament prophecy that included Gentiles under the wonderful saving grace of God. And Peter was chosen to receive the first revelation of this new dimension of grace. He responded much like we respond when God begins to give a new vision of His purposes in the earth. He rejected it on the grounds that it was unscriptural, according to his current paradigm. He was bound to a limited understanding of the Scriptures.

It was very difficult for Peter to make this transition to another dimension of faith and revelation. Similarly, it will require a painful paradigm shift for Christians to move into the realm of the supernatural that requires us to simply believe these words of Jesus: "Most assuredly, I say to you, he who believes in Me, the works that I do he will do also; and greater works than these he will do, because I go to My Father" (John 14:12). Oswald Chambers wrote, "Prayer does not fit us for greater works—it is the greater work."[1]

TRUE SPIRITUAL MINISTRY

Yonggi Cho gives us a picture of ministry in the fourth dimension:

> I cannot carry out my ministry of winning souls by simply knocking on doors, struggling and working myself to death. I use the way of faith and the church is growing by leaps and bounds. And even though I have a church of over 50,000 members [today it is 850,000!] when I go

to the office I do not have a great deal to do, for I am following a path of faith and am not constantly striving in my flesh to bring to pass those things that the Holy Spirit can easily do.[2]

The "way of faith" to which Dr. Cho refers demands that we believe the scriptural explanation that "faith is the substance of things hoped for, the evidence of things not seen" (Heb. 11:1). The way of faith does not accept what is seen in the third dimension—our natural circumstances—if it is contrary to the vision and dream we have received from the fourth dimension—the realm of the Spirit.

"I use the way of faith and the church is growing by leaps and bounds."—Dr. Cho

---

Of course, the Scriptures relate to the supernatural realm of the Spirit, for God is Spirit. Believing God's Word requires us to live and minister in the fourth dimension, allowing our redeemed spirit to become a channel for the moving of the Spirit of God. Then our lives become empowered by the gifts of the Holy Spirit as well as the language of the Spirit, such as prophecy, dreams, and visions. Through supernatural revelation of God's Word, which is His will for our lives, we can have dominion over the third dimension and bring the manifestation of the Kingdom of God to the earth.

The Scriptures, both Old and New Testaments, are replete with experiences of people who encountered the spiritual world. They experienced dreams, visions, trances, hearing the audible voice of God, and even being translated—caught away by the Spirit—like Philip experienced after he ministered to the Ethiopian eunuch (see Acts 8). Moses saw God in a burning bush. The glory cloud and the pillar of fire were visible to the Israelites as they journeyed in the wilderness, and the apostle Paul referred to visits to Heaven, just to name a few.

In the Old Testament, the word *prophet* is used 300 times; in the New Testament it is used 100 times. The prophetic ministry, which involves dreams and visions, the gift of prophecy, and the office of a prophet, is a realm of spiritual realities. Through the prophetic anointing we proclaim what we have seen in the fourth dimension and we understand what God wants to do in a specific situation. We receive faith to declare the Word of God and see it manifested in reality.

As he followed the way of faith, Yonggi Cho began to make prophetic announcements. He simply began to say what God had promised in His Word. Then God began to give him specific words of knowledge and prophetic dreams regarding His divine purpose for building a church in Korea. What has become the world's largest church was not built with promotional skills, wealthy sponsors, or even polished worship teams. It was built by men and women learning to walk in the fourth dimension spiritual realities. They have learned to pray in such a way that these spiritual realities were manifest in the third dimension, where many souls could be delivered from satan's power and brought to salvation through Jesus Christ.

Delivered From Knowing Too Much

The enemy would like to keep us from knowing that God is very willing to move miraculously among us today just as He did in the early Church. I was enjoying dinner with Pastor

Augustine Degorl, a minister from Ghana who preached at our church, when he startled me with a question. He asked, "Did I ever tell you about the man I raised from the dead?" I replied calmly, "No, I don't recall that you have." I am aware of numerous accounts of people being raised from the dead in Africa and India. Yet, it has a greater impact when you hear the account from the person God used to perform such an outstanding miracle.

They only knew what Jesus did and what He told His disciples to do—so they did it.

This African pastor began to explain that, as a teenager, he was part of a powerful revival that touched many young people in his area. He and his friends would get together to pray. Not having fine facilities as we do in this country, they would simply take their machetes and cut out a clearing in the jungle to have a place to pray together. In that jungle "cathedral," these young people spent hours calling on God, telling Him they wanted to be His servants and to do His work in the earth.

Understanding only the basic gospel message from the New Testament, Pastor Augustine and his friends began to do what they read in the Scriptures. When they would come out from their place of prayer, they would go to homes and lay hands on the sick and pray for them. They saw many miraculous healings. On one occasion, they went to the local hospital to pray for the patients. Everyone they prayed for was healed; they actually emptied out the local hospital![3]

They could only read the Gospels because they didn't know how to understand the rest of the Bible and had no teachers. *They only knew what Jesus did and what He told His disciples to do—so they did it.* They had no intellectual theologian to tell them that the age of miracles was past or that healing was only for the age of the apostles. And because they had never attended a neatly packaged, one hour long church service, they didn't know that the many hours they spent together in prayer in the jungle were "inordinately long." They actually thought they should do what Jesus said when He sent out His disciples: "Cast out demons and heal diseases" (see Luke 9:1; 10:1). They believed the Scriptures that taught they were supposed to go to people's homes and ask who was sick in the home so they could pray for their healing (see Luke 10:9).

Remember, the Kingdom of God exists in the reality of the fourth dimension. These young African believers thought they should heal the sick and say, "The kingdom of God has come near to you" (Luke 10:9). Since they believed the Word that said they had *authority* over devils and diseases, they went to the local hospital and got a list of the sicknesses and diseases of the patients including those in ICU. Because they *believed* they had authority over diseases, freeing the people from them was not difficult—from their perspective of the fourth dimension.

"On one occasion," Pastor Augustine continued, "I came to a place where a young man had died the night before. I found the villagers all weeping and wailing, crying out to false gods to make him live again. I went into the room where the dead man had lain all night and the next day. After praying about 20 minutes, I remembered the Gospel account of Jesus raising a young girl from the dead and saying, "Young girl, arise." So I said to the dead man, "Young man, arise."

When I said these words, the man's foot began to move. Then his eyes opened and when he looked at me he was very frightened, not knowing what had happened. I simply took him by the hand and led him out into the village. As a result of this miracle, many people believed in Jesus and accepted Him as their Savior, just as they did in Jesus' day when Lazarus was raised from the dead.

"So I said to the dead man, 'Young man, arise.'"

It is unfortunate that, in our theology, we have decided *what* God won't do or doesn't do today. We desperately need to be delivered from "knowing too much." To know more than the Scriptures teach is heresy. What we do not seem to realize is that the devil has managed to use our intellectual approach to life in the third dimension to keep from us the true information of what God is doing today—in the fourth dimension. The Kingdom of God is a spiritual kingdom of faith that belongs to those who learn to live and minister in the fourth dimension.

THE REAL JESUS

My African friend, Pastor Augustine, had read the Gospels exclusively long enough to discover the real Jesus—the compassionate Son of Man who heals the sick and casts out devils. He learned to know the Jesus who declared, "The Spirit of the Lord is upon Me, because He has anointed Me to preach the gospel to the poor; He has sent Me to heal the brokenhearted, to proclaim liberty to the captives and recovery of sight to the blind, to set at liberty those who are oppressed; to proclaim the acceptable year of the Lord" (Luke 4:18-19). He had never been taught to be disobedient to Jesus' instructions to heal the sick and cast out devils. His simple understanding of the gospel taught him that "to love Jesus is to do what He told us to do."

When Jesus walked the earth, He showed how much He loved people by healing them and casting out their devils. Then He instructed His followers to do the same. He promised that they would do the works He did, and even greater works, because He went to His Father (see John 14:12). Jesus expects believers to do what He did—and even more. If we decide to live and minister in the fourth dimension, the pathway of faith, we can be used by God to bring His saving and healing power to hurting and needy people wherever we are.

Jesus showed how much He loved people by healing them and casting out devils.

Norvel Hayes shared with me how his daughter was healed and then saved. It is a thrilling example of how a father, through faith alone, declaring the promises of God's Word, could bring the supernatural power of the fourth dimension into his daughter's situation. He explained that his daughter, Zona, felt she had the ugliest arms and legs in the school. She was embarrassed about the large, unsightly, festering boils—42 of them—that covered her skin. He prayed and prayed for her to be healed. Then one day, Pastor Hayes described his experience in prayer, saying, "The Lord took me into a cloud in His presence. In that awesome place, I heard the voice of the Lord say to me, 'How long are you going to allow your daughter to be sick?'"

"I protested, 'She's the one allowing it. I'm praying for her.' In an authoritative voice the Lord spoke again, 'You're her father. You are not praying correctly. Stop asking Me if I will heal your daughter. Curse the unsightly growths on your daughter's body. *Curse* the very root of those boils in My name and they will die and disappear. After you curse them, *declare* that she is free from boils, knots, and growths. Then, *thank* Me for removing them.'"

"So I changed my pitiful pleading with the Lord to heal my daughter. For 40 days, I cursed the boils that were infecting my daughter's body. There seemed to be no change, but I kept insisting that this affliction was cursed in the name of Jesus, and thanking God for destroying them. Then one day Zona came running into my room, calling to me, 'Daddy, Daddy, look at me, look at me!' Startled, I looked up from my work and saw that my daughter's skin was normal, soft and beautiful—every boil and wart had disappeared." The spiritual reality of the fourth dimension authority had swallowed up the third dimension problem.

I changed my pitiful pleading with the Lord to heal my daughter.

The battle for Zona's life and destiny continued, however. She later married a man who served in the military in Vietnam. He wrote a letter to Zona from Vietnam that she misunderstood as a "Dear John" letter, perceiving that he was telling her good-bye forever. She thought she would never see him again. As a result of this heartbreaking experience, Zona began to run with a wild crowd, hanging out in bars and taking drugs. For three years her father prayed for her desperately to be delivered and restored to relationship with her family and her God.

Pastor Hayes recounted to me that one day while staying in their home, Zona came running into her father's room again, ecstatic and terrified. She fairly screamed, "Daddy, there is a huge angel in my room!" Her father told her it was her guardian angel. She said, "But I don't want such a big angel. I'm terrified!" Heaven had gotten her attention. In the following weeks, God worked miracles of restoration, bringing her husband back to her, and establishing their Christian marriage.

Zona had become anorexic, in addition to her problem with drug addiction, and doctors said she could never become pregnant. Yet, she miraculously conceived and gave birth to a beautiful, normal baby. Zona is now the chief executive for her father's entire ministry. Her wonderful testimony is also included in Norvel Hayes's book, *Pleasing the Lord*.[4] The real Jesus wants to bring His miraculous power of the fourth dimension into our third dimension lives. And He has ordained that we become channels of spiritual blessing for the lives of others as well.

Endnotes

1. Oswald Chambers, *My Utmost for His Highest*, as quoted in *My Utmost Devotional Bible* (Nashville, TN: Thomas Nelson Publishers, 1992), p. 1205.

2. Dr. David Yonggi Cho, *The Fourth Dimension* (Gainesville, FL: Bridge-Logos, 1979).

3. Augustine Degorl, Pastor of Throne Room Worship Center, 7114 Fabian Court, Houston, TX 77083.

4. Norvel Hayes, *Pleasing the Lord* (Cleveland, TN: Norvel Hayes Ministries, 1997).

CHAPTER 6

FAITH AND CULTURE

Receiving the Truth

Faith is as universal as the truth of salvation through Jesus Christ. Missionaries have taken the good news of the gospel throughout the world to kings and cannibals, with the same miraculous response. I have preached the truth of God's Word to emotional Frenchmen, to reserved Germans, to responsive New Zealanders. I have taken the same wonderful message of faith in Christ to the oppressed, poverty-ridden people of India and to the exuberant, colorful culture of Latin America. It has been my experience that when the Spirit of God breaks through on the hearts of people with His supernatural power, *culture is not a hindrance to receiving the truth of God's Word*. When the Holy Spirit does His wonderful convicting work, the third dimension of any culture gives way to the revelation of faith in Christ—in the spiritual realm.

The spiritual breakthrough that many nations have received has released congregations into a *lifestyle* of prayer. These powerful revival fires have ushered them into a functioning reality of flowing in the gifts of the Spirit and has changed the focus and purpose of believers' lives. The priority of corporate prayer has resulted in a manifestation of the supernatural, miraculous work of the Holy Spirit, even on a national level. Entire nations are being transformed through this wonderful revival.

For example, according to surveys, Uganda had one of the worst African AIDS epidemics in the early 1990s. The Christians in Uganda have encouraged their nation to promote abstinence and monogamy among the people. Christian leaders have prayed and taught Christian family values, and influenced their government policy. Researchers report that Uganda's approach to AIDS prevention was "unusual." Concerned men and women worked their way into communities through "local networks of village meetings, chiefs, musicians, churches and care groups. The approach seemed to work, according to surveys that suggest that casual sex dropped by 60 percent between 1989 and 1995, which led to a great reduction in HIV rates."[1]

Samuel Lee is an Iranian pastor, who converted to Christianity from Islam. His church in Amsterdam, Holland, is predominantly Nigerian and Ghanaian. He is training immigrants from Africa, Asia, and the Middle East to reach the nations of Europe. He warns against trying to build a church with stylish buildings, promoting social gatherings, and missing the Holy Spirit's agenda. He declares, "We must be careful, lest we become like the unwise virgins who had their lamps yet forgot to bring oil—and the door was shut for them. We must embrace the miraculous. We need the Holy Spirit like never before."[2]

My point is this. We sometimes attribute the spiritual breakthroughs and prayer lifestyles we are witnessing in other nations to the idea that it "fits" their culture. In doing that, we unwittingly exclude our culture from the same opportunity for breakthrough. Differences in culture simply do not hinder, or aid, the revelation of God's power in the fourth dimension. It is the power of the Holy Spirit alone that brings the light of the Kingdom of God into our third dimension darkness. Those who have been given eyes to see the wonderful realities of the fourth dimension through powerful prayer lifestyles are bringing those realities into manifestation in their lives, churches, and nations. Jesus said,

The lamp of the body is the eye. If therefore your eye is good, your whole body will be full of light. But if your eye is bad, your whole body will be full of darkness. If therefore the light that is in you is darkness, how great is that darkness! (Matthew 6:22-23)

As we observe the dynamic within the spiritual community where wonderful miracles and great ingathering of souls are happening, we see a predominance of unusual prayer and faith working in believers. Prayer has opened their eyes to receive by faith the promises of God. They have an understanding of how to activate the power and authority to obtain these divine promises. Based on this observation, a pastor friend of mine said, "If I ever become seriously ill, just throw me over into a bunch of Nigerians and ask them to pray for me." Of course, Africans don't have a corner on receiving the promises of God. The wonderful, supernatural power of prayer is available to everyone. But the African Christians definitely have a handle on receiving the promises of God through commitment to prayer. They understand the authority in the words of the apostle Peter, who declared:

> *...His divine power has given to us all things that pertain to life and godliness, through the knowledge of Him who called us by glory and virtue, by which have been given to us exceedingly great and precious promises, that through these you may be partakers of the divine nature, having escaped the corruption that is in the world through lust* (2 Peter 1:3-4).

---

*Most megachurches in **Europe** have been raised up by **African** pastors.*

To demonstrate further that this supernatural move of God, which is known for miracles and a phenomenal harvest of souls, does not reflect a cultural paradigm, consider this: Most megachurches in *Europe* have been raised up by *African* pastors. While many of us rushed through the window of opportunity in the former Soviet Union and rejoiced to have a part in reaping that great harvest, these African apostles stayed to establish churches.

I was among those who invested ministry into Ukraine, traveling there on several occasions. Our church sent a weekly TV program into Kharkov for two years afterward, teaching the basic truths of the gospel. Yet, it gave me pause when "suddenly" there appeared on the horizon an African apostle named Sunday Adelaja. He established a church of 30,000 in Kiev,

Ukraine—the largest church in Europe. Our church had sent teams to Ukraine on short missions trips. We rejoiced in winning several thousand converts to the Lord. But Sunday Adelaja established a church there, and a huge one at that. His testimony is that this megachurch was established through the power of prayer:

> In our church in Ukraine, we have a 24-hour prayer chain and prayer from 11 P.M. to 6 A.M. every night. Additionally, we hold a three-day time of fasting and prayer on the last weekend of each month.[3]

Establishing a lifestyle of prayer for all believers is the key to the power and growth of these phenomenal churches. As American Christians, the way we relate to these supernatural happenings in other nations will be very important to our lives and ministries in the next few years. Joseph D'souza, who heads the All India Christian Council, wisely observes:

> The American church has ignored the fact that it is no longer the epicenter of global Christianity. The activity of the Church has shifted to the Southern Hemisphere. Soon we will see an increase in the number of full-time Christian workers coming from the developing world to do evangelism and church planting in the United States. It is high time the American church, in conjunction with other nations, finds a way to work in partnership with those nations so that together, as equals, we all may praise the Lord of the harvest for all He has done.[4]

Although faith is not cultural, there can be a mentality—a paradigm—in cultures that negates the Lordship of Christ over our lives. Remember, we can only learn to pray in another dimension when we receive revelation that another dimension exists as an eternal reality. Jackson Senyonga, who pastors a church of 40,000 in Uganda, observes that the American church is more program-oriented than "presence-oriented." He contrasts this tendency to the African church, which "is not drawn to programs but to the presence of God that overwhelms hearts, changes lives and empowers people. The African church exists in the realm of the miraculous because of ongoing, fervent prayer." Senyonga seriously indicts the American church, which "has no time for God." For this reason, he continues, "The American church suffers from prayerlessness."[5]

A lifestyle of prayer is the key to the power and growth of these phenomenal churches.

The prayer ministry in other nations is not culture-driven; it is faith and need driven. One Ghanaian pastor told me that prayer had always been a way of life for him. He stated simply, "We pray to survive. We pray to protect ourselves from the shaman and the witch doctor. We pray for something to eat so we will not starve. We learned how to pray and receive healing from God because there were no hospitals or doctors. Prayer has never been an option; it is our lifeline." Perhaps, in this sense, the affluence of our American culture does play a negative role in our failure to live in fourth dimension realities. Our prosperous lifestyle robs us of a sense of dependence on God to provide for our temporal necessities.

African Christians also have the strong sense that they must be obedient servants of God, committed to the harvest of souls in the nations—fulfilling the Great Commission. They know that they can only accomplish this high calling through prayer. Therefore, as they obediently reach out to reap the harvest, they continually touch the miraculous power of God through fervent, consistent praying.

The African church exists in a realm of the miraculous because of ongoing fervent prayer.

It is not my intention to disparage the genuine work of God at present in our nation. On the contrary, my desire is that the Holy Spirit will shine His light in our hearts, filling us with zeal for the presence of God to be manifest in our lives and churches in a more powerful dimension of prayer. We can allow the wonderful work of God in other nations to make us "zealous for good works" (Titus 2:14). As we allow God to change our cultural and religious paradigm, and to prepare a new wineskin for the outpouring of the Holy Spirit, we can expect to see a wonderful end-time revival in our churches and our nation.

ENDNOTES

1. "Uganda Sees Stunning Decline in AIDS Cases," Health on the Net Foundation, found on the Internet at http://www.hon.ch/News/HSN/518674.html, accessed Dec. 27, 2005.

2. Kevin Turner, "Why Isn't the American Church Growing?" *Charisma* (Lake Mary, FL: Strang Communications, January 2005).

3. Ibid., Sunday Adelaja.

4. Ibid., Joseph D'souza.

5.   Ibid., Jackson Senyonga.

CHAPTER 7

NEW WINESKINS

Preserving New Life

Jesus acknowledged the fact that it is unnatural for human nature to quickly accept change, to relinquish the old and familiar for the new. Yet, He emphasized the need for change, illustrated by a parable about a familiar item to all Jews—a wineskin:

> *And no one puts new wine into old wineskins; or else the new wine will burst the wineskins and be spilled, and the wineskins will be ruined. But new wine must be put into new wineskins, and both are preserved. And no one, having drunk old wine, immediately desires new; for he says, 'The old is better'"* (Luke 5:37-39).

In this parable, Jesus addressed an inherent weakness of human nature: resistance to change. We sometimes say we want "something new" in God and that we are tired of the old. But when the time comes to make the necessary paradigm shift to receive fresh divine revelation, we often find that we have become comfortable with—more accurately, in bondage to—the old and familiar. We protect ourselves from the risk involved in change, especially when it seems unpredictable and unfamiliar.

WILLINGNESS TO CHANGE

But Jesus understood that the only way to receive the new wine—which is symbolic of the work of the Holy Spirit in our lives—was to prepare a new wineskin. Otherwise, He warned, we could expect to burst the wineskin and lose the wine. Applying the analogy, we understand that not being willing to prepare our hearts for change will result in "tearing up the church" and disempowering the prayer effort.

*We protect ourselves
from the risk involved in change.*

Jesus' conclusion of the matter is that "new wine must be put into new wineskins, and both are preserved" (Luke 5:38). If believers allow themselves to become new wineskins, both the wineskins (our hearts) and the wine (the Holy Spirit) will be safely preserved, allowing the work of the Holy Spirit to go forward.

It is quite apparent that God is in the process of preparing new wineskins for the new wine He is getting ready to pour out on His Church. He is radically changing believers and entire churches, preparing them to be filled with new wine. Bart Pierce cites Africa as the "midwife" of the next prayer movement in the earth. He has ministered in Africa to a convention of between 4 million and 6 million at one time. They come to "church" to pray fervently and receive what they need from God.

There is a word in the Swahili African language, *emogeni*, which means "getting into the Spirit." The African believers state simply, "We go to church so that together we can get to where we are going." They expect to experience the supernatural power of God in their services. Contrast that mind-set with a typical American mentality of attending church. According to George Barna, author of *Boiling Point*,[1] most Americans attending church on Sunday leave the service dissatisfied, feeling an empty sense of futility. Many churches present several different types of programs every Sunday morning in an effort to appeal to different age groups. And pastors dare not plan more than one hour for the entire service for most people to "endure." In contrast, these praying African believers come together for many hours to "go somewhere" through the power of real prayer. They call on the Lord with one voice and experience miracles of healing, deliverance, and divine help for every life situation.

One of the main problems with prayer in America is that it is not working. Another major problem is that Christians are not praying. Some spiritual leaders predict that if this situation does not change, within five years the American church will evaporate off the scene of influence over our culture. Duncan-Williams told our congregation:

> If the church doesn't rise up to pray, the enemy will take over. The devil wants to kill you. If you pray, you will become un-kill-able and un-die-able. The more time

you spend with God in prayer, the less time you will have with the devil in problems. Make up your mind to "push" as a woman in travail. It is too dangerous to stop praying. Keep it going until we get out of here. The enemy will test praying people more than other people.

RESPONSIBILITY OF A HOUSE OF PRAYER

God is pouring out the new wine of *prayer in another dimension*, which is transforming entire nations. As believers in our nation, we can yield to the power of the Holy Spirit to enter into this new dimension of prayer. Then revelation will come regarding the prophetic promises of God for us as individuals, churches, and a nation. It is the work of the believer to pray these promises into manifestation as we prepare our lives to become new wineskins, filled with the power of the Holy Spirit. We must be willing to "push" until we see the breakthrough in prayer that God wants to give to us for revival and a harvest of souls.

God is pouring out the new wine of
prayer in another dimension*.*

There is a divine responsibility to the people who are called to be a house of prayer. The biblical pattern, which is required to develop an atmosphere of prayer for all nations, is seen throughout the Old and New Testaments. When Solomon finished the house of the Lord, he offered prayers of dedication and repentance to the Lord in the presence of the whole nation.

The Scripture declares: "Solomon successfully accomplished all that came into his heart to make in the house of the Lord..." (2 Chron. 7:11b). It was then that the Lord manifested His presence:

Then the Lord appeared to Solomon by night, and said to him: "I have heard your prayer, and have chosen this place for Myself as a house of sacrifice. When I shut up Heaven and there is no rain, or command the locusts to devour the land, or send pestilence among My people, if My people who are called by My name will humble themselves, and pray and seek My face, and turn from their wicked ways, then I will hear from Heaven, and will forgive their sin and heal their land. Now My eyes will be open and My ears attentive to prayer made in this place. For now, I have chosen and sanctified this house, that My name may be there forever; and My eyes and My heart will be there perpetually" (2 Chronicles 7:12-16).

Into this atmosphere saturated with prayer, God chose to come to dwell perpetually in that place, sanctifying this earthly temple and putting His name there forever. What an awesome thought! God called Solomon's temple a "house of sacrifice." That was characteristic of a house of prayer, for the law of Moses required that sacrifices be offered on the altar along with prayers of supplication. The reward for building a house of sacrifice was to have the name of God, His eyes, and His heart dwell there forever. It was not for Solomon's name to be great, or the people's. It was for the presence of God to dwell among His people—perpetually.

GET OUR LIVES RIGHT

In 1904, God moved so mightily in the nation of Wales that one-third of the nation's citizens were radically transformed by the gospel of Jesus Christ. Taverns and red-light districts in cities were completely shut down, as their participants found the saving power of Christ and attended church instead. Following the biblical pattern, Evan Roberts and other men of God in Wales had saturated themselves with prayer and intercession for their nation. They prepared an atmosphere in which God was pleased to dwell. The Lord showed these leaders that to maintain this powerful revival they were responsible to follow these four steps of faith:

1. Obey the Spirit promptly.

2. Confess Christ publicly.

3. Put away unconfessed sin.

4. Put away doubtful habits.[2]

In short, these praying Christians understood that they had to get their lives right before God, just as God had spoken to Solomon. The four steps God required of His nation Israel in order for them to have His presence were: (1) humble themselves, (2) pray, (3) seek His face, (4) turn from their wicked ways (see 2 Chron. 7:14). Considering Evan Roberts's list of requirements along with this biblical injunction, we can summarize that our responsibility for experiencing revival involves seeking God in prayer and getting our lives right, reconciled to His will.

Every revival recorded in history has been the result of continued, intense, travailing prayer. God's promise to break through on His people is based on divine conditions; He will come on His terms. Revivals don't come by preaching; they come by prayer. The purpose of preaching is to get people to call on God.

True prayer requires expending vital energy. It is the highest effort of which the human spirit is capable. God desires to move among us, but He requires that we get our lives right with Him and engage Him in fervent prayer. Into that atmosphere, the omnipotent power of God can move mightily, transforming lives and situations for His glory.

PURPOSE OF OUR OBEDIENCE

Our loving heavenly Father wants us to be reconciled in obedience to Him in every area of our lives so that He can bless us. God wants to bless us now, in the future, and throughout eternity. When God called Abram to leave his land and all that was familiar to him, it was so that He could bless Abram. He promised to multiply his seed as the stars of heaven, and cause him to be a blessing to many nations.

It is difficult to imagine that Abraham had such an intimate, obedient relationship with the living God before there was a Bible, before the law of God was even given. Yet, as Enoch and Noah had done before him, Abram heard and heeded the voice of God. His personal encounter with God imparted to him a willingness to leave his home and become a nomad, wandering the earth in search of a "city which has foundations, whose builder and maker is God" (Heb. 11:10). It is God's desire to bless His people and to accomplish His divine will of redemption through them. But first He has to know that He can trust us to obey Him. He is not interested in simply making us quit doing things we want to do. His command to obedience is because He wants to bless us and make us a blessing to others. For that reason we need to be willing for change.

Evan Roberts taught believers: "It will be no good getting thousands to the churches unless we learn the lesson of obedience to the Spirit. If I had not given up everything to the Spirit, I would not be here today. Though the whole world sneer at me, I know I must obey the Spirit."[3] In order to pray in another dimension and experience the revival fires of God, obedience to God must become a way of life. We will need to become new wineskins that can contain the new wine of revival without bursting. All hidden sin must be washed away by the precious blood of Jesus. And we will need to receive divine revelation of the biblical pattern of prayer in another dimension.

ENDNOTES

1. George Barna, *Boiling Point* (Ventura, CA: Regal Books, 2001).

2. Eifion Evans, *The Welsh Revival of 1904* (Bridgend, Mid Glamorgan, Wales: Bryntirion Press, Evangelical Press of Wales, 1987), pp. 166-67.

3. Ibid.

CHAPTER 8

PRAYING IN ANOTHER DIMENSION

The Biblical Pattern

I n the nations where God is moving mightily, it is normal for believers to be involved in continual prayer, corporately and individually. You can go to their sanctuaries at any hour of the day or night and find believers praying. Their churches have truly become what Jesus ordained them to be: "a house of prayer for all nations." They have embraced the biblical pattern of prayer, which has unlocked the power of God into their lives. And their hearts have truly become temples of God, committed to a lifestyle of prayer.

COMMITMENT TO PRAYER

Do you realize that the nation of Israel was accustomed to praying three times a day as their regular prayer lifestyle? Daniel prayed three times a day. The psalmist David declared:

"*Evening and morning and at noon I will pray, and cry aloud, and He shall hear my voice. He has redeemed my soul in peace from the battle that was against me*" (Ps. 55:17-18a). And fire came down from Heaven when Elijah prayed at the evening hour of prayer.

This biblical pattern of daily prayer was maintained in the lives of the early Church. We read in the Book of Acts that Peter and John were going to the temple at the hour of prayer when they healed the lame man at the Gate Beautiful. It was the first hour of prayer when the Holy Spirit fell on the day of Pentecost. And it was the hour of prayer when Peter went up to the rooftop to pray and had his revelation to take the good news to the Gentiles. In the Book of Acts we read that the Church gathered daily in prayer: "*So continuing daily with one accord in the temple, and breaking bread from house to house, they ate their food with gladness and simplicity of heart*" (Acts 2:46).

Even today, practicing Jews pray three times a day, and Muslims respond to a call to prayer five times a day. While ministering in India, I was awakened at 5:30 A.M. by the Muslim call to prayer. To this day I can hear the haunting, mournful cry of that call, to which an entire population responds, halting all activity to pray to their god.

When he prayed to Jesus, he was keenly aware that Someone was there, listening.

One former Muslim testified that he had prayed over 5,600 hours to Allah. When He found Jesus as His true Savior, he rejoiced at the great difference his personal relationship with

Christ made in prayer. When he prayed to Jesus, he was keenly aware that Someone was there, listening. Yet, even in his religious darkness, he had been committed to prayer to fulfill his obligation to Allah. As a Christian, this established prayer commitment could now serve him well, as he learned to enter into the presence of the living God through prayer.

Old Testament Pattern

God promised Old Testament saints: *"Call to Me, and I will answer you, and show you great and mighty things, which you do not know"* (Jer. 33:3). The word *call* translated here is the Hebrew word *qará*, which implies "accosting a person, crying out to them, properly calling them by name" (Strong's #7121). It involves perseverance, determination, commitment, and inner tenacity. Such fervent prayer brings revelation of God's will into specific situations that can only be changed through prayer.

Today, nations are being influenced by the power of prophetic prayer.

History records the exploits of great men and women of prayer. Queen Victoria of England, in the pomp and power of her reign declared: "I fear nothing except the prayers of John Knox." The Englishman, Reese Howells, a mighty intercessor, prayed earnestly during World War II for his nation. He announced that the Germans would not invade England. However, when they began their invasion, Howells went back to God in fervent prayer. It was then that Hitler aborted his planned invasion of England, sending the troops to Russia instead.

Today, nations are being influenced as well by the power of prophetic prayer and declaration. Archbishop Duncan-Williams prophesied that a certain general would be elected the next president of Nigeria. Many found it hard to believe him because that general had already been president 20 years earlier. However, it happened as he had prophesied it would. The nation elected this veteran general again to be president of Nigeria. God reveals His plans to those who intercede for His will in the nations.

New Testament Pattern

The Book of the Acts of the Apostles reveals a deep commitment of the early Church to a lifestyle of fervent prayer. The apostles established their lives on prayer and the reading of the Word, delegating the serving of tables to other good men, full of the Holy Spirit and wisdom (see Acts 6). Stephen, one of those servers, who also did great wonders and signs among the people (see Acts 6:8), prayed for his murderers when they stoned him to death, making him a martyr for the gospel. These early Christians prayed for their enemies, for protection, for boldness, for deliverance; they prayed together and when they were alone. They prayed consistently, several times a day.

Christians who do great things and have great power with God are people who are deeply committed to prayer. Dr. Yonggi Cho sets aside three times a day for prayer. Before ministering in the pulpit, he prays for three hours. When ministering in Japan, he prays for six hours before preaching. He has established a place called "Prayer Mountain, where people go to stay in tiny grottoes alone for days and weeks at time to pray and fast. There are 25,000 people praying there every day, and this has been continuing for over 20 years. Again, Duncan-Williams admonishes believers:

> If you want to see the miracles of God, commit yourself to prayer like crazy. Make prayer a lifestyle. Commit to it until you die. The reason we don't have miracles in the church today is that we don't pray. Take it up to another level. Apply more pressure to the enemy. Make up your mind to "push" to birth the purposes of God. When you feel the pain of travail, don't stop praying.[1]

My friend, Bishop Bart Pierce pastors Rock City Church in Baltimore, Maryland.[2] He made this general comparison from what he observed among the Africans: "They do not sit when they pray; they stand. They walk, they get loud, they pray with fervor. In contrast, my observation of American Christians in prayer meetings is that they want to sit, be quiet, and not use energy or show strong emotion."

"If you want to see the miracles of God, commit yourself to prayer like crazy."—Duncan-Williams

---

As American Christians, we desperately need a paradigm shift concerning our commitment to prayer. The church's biblical purpose for existing is to become a house of prayer. Therefore, every believer must make a commitment to fulfill that purpose. Otherwise, the church will not be a dwelling place for the presence and power of God we so desperately need. Souls cannot be saved without that divine power. Personal destiny cannot be realized without it. Neither can the enemy of our souls be vanquished without the supernatural power of God.

BIBLICAL PRAYER PATTERNS

Until I began to teach American believers regarding prayer in another dimension, I personally did not realize how committed we are to our traditional attitudes. We are opposed to changing even our postures and approaches to prayer, many of which are not biblical. Bart Pierce concluded that in America too often we have allowed *religious* people to establish the environment for our prayer ministry. Religious tradition is one step away from reality, preferring form and familiarity to fervor and function. While our traditions allow us a feeling of religious satisfaction, they fall short of bringing effective results in the lives and situations of hurting people.

When Bart Pierce ministered at our church, one of our more astute members made this observation concerning his manner of praying: "I don't think I have ever seen anyone pray as fervently, without ceasing, as Pastor Pierce did during our pre-service prayer. His intense focus was impressive." According to Pierce, there are at least five specific characteristics of the kind of prayer Africans engage in that makes their lives and churches so powerful. He observed the following elements in the prayers of the Africans that help them pray in another dimension:

1. Their prayers are *vocal*, rather than silent.

2. They pray *fervently*, focused on specific needs.

3. They consistently pray the Word—*through proclamation.*

4. Their entire focus is *vertical*, addressing God alone.

5. Their prayers are full of the authority of a *prophetic* anointing.[3]

I began to study the biblical foundation for each of these characteristics of prayer—vocal, fervent, proclaiming the Word, vertical, prophetic—that characterize the powerful prayer lives of believers in other nations. As I did, what became very clear, by contrast, was the lack of energy, focus, authority, and prophetic anointing that characterizes much of the praying in our American churches. If we learn to yield our hearts and minds (our old wineskins) to biblical patterns of prayer, we can begin to see the power of God released in our churches and our nation, just as these precious Christians in other nations have experienced. The prayer lives of Christians in these revival nations closely resemble the fervency of the Old Testament prophets as well as the New Testament Church.

Our church is on a quest to establish ourselves in the kind of powerful prayer life we are observing in other nations. We want to see the same proportions of harvest of souls, the kinds of healing and multiplied miracles, even to the raising of the dead, as God is doing in these revival nations. It is time for American churches to take a quantum leap into prayer in another dimension. We need to learn to use prayer as a weapon against the onslaught of the enemy, who continues to "steal, kill, and destroy" (see John 10:10). He continually attacks the spiritual lives and integrity of our families, our churches, and our nation. We must insist on the victory of Calvary and bring the Kingdom of God to earth through powerful, persistent prayer.

FIVE SMOOTH STONES

It is time for American churches to take a quantum leap into prayer in another dimension.

Until we grasp the fact that the essence of true prayer is *spiritual* and must be accomplished through the Holy Spirit working effectively in our spiritual life, we will not enter into another dimension of prayer. We have to lay aside intellectual prayers, based on facts and knowledge. Analyzing situations and explaining them to God is a futile attempt to pray. God's perspective of life is much different from ours. We cannot pray effectively if we are filled with strife and complaint or other negative emotional responses. We must learn to abandon ourselves in complete trust and confidence in God, who has given us the recourse of prayer to present our petitions in faith to Him.

Jesus made it very clear to His disciples that He wanted them to *ask*, to *seek*, and to *knock*, to receive answers to prayer (see Luke 11:9). He declared: *"And in that day you will ask Me nothing. Most assuredly, I say to you, whatever you ask the Father in My name He will give you. Until now you have asked nothing in My name. Ask, and you will receive, that your joy may be full"* (John 16:23-24).

My dear friend, Dr. Fuchsia Pickett, shared with me on one occasion a spiritual vision God gave her in which He taught her how to use spiritual weapons of warfare. She was an avid student of the Word of God, as a Methodist professor, before she was miraculously healed from her deathbed and baptized with the Holy Spirit. She had not believed in either the reality of healing for the Church today or Holy Spirit baptism—until she received both on the same morning. Then God began to teach her His ways, as she yielded her strong intellect as well as her theological degrees to Him. She learned to approach God in the simplicity of a child. Dr. Pickett recorded this vision in her book, *Stones of Remembrance*,[4] which I have summarized here:

> I was praying before I went to bed and the Lord spoke to me, "If you will spend the night with Me, as the day dawns I will teach you how to have power over the devil." …Just as the dawn came, I fell into a trance and began to see a young man with broad shoulders and a ruddy face. He had a shepherd's sling draped over his shoulder. As I looked at him, I said, "You are David." Then I began to watch a drama unfold. As David reached into the brook at his feet and picked up five stones, I saw a huge person walk into the other side of the room. I looked up, startled by his size, and whispered, "You are Goliath." Then I saw David put four stones away and sling one stone at the giant. The Holy Spirit asked me, "In what authority did he sling that rock?" I remembered David's words to Goliath: "…but I come to you in the name of the Lord of Hosts" (1 Sam. 17:45).
>
> I watched in the vision as Goliath fell when David's smooth stone found its mark in his forehead. Then I became a part of the vision, as the Holy Spirit said, "Now, you take the other four stones and place them in your sling." Now I had to use these stones to defeat the enemy. First, the Holy Spirit asked me, "What stone did Jesus

throw at the devil?" I answered, "Jesus' response to the devil was 'It is written.'" Then I hurled the stone of the Word at the enemy. Then the Spirit asked me, "What is the line the enemy cannot cross?" I responded, "The blood of Jesus. That is what the Passover was all about." And I hurled the second stone. Then I heard the question, "What is the source of your strength for battle?" I responded, "It is 'not by might, nor by power, but by My spirit, saith the Lord of hosts'" (Zech. 4:6 [KJV]). I understood that this stone represented the power of the Holy Spirit. Finally, the Holy Spirit asked, "Whose faith is it?" And I responded with the words of Paul, "The life which I now live in the flesh I live by the faith of the Son of God" (Gal. 2:20 [KJV]). I understood that defeating the enemy is not about standing and yelling and stomping our feet. It involves using the divine arsenal of weapons God has given us—the name of the Lord, His Word, His blood, the power of His Spirit, and His faith. Then the Holy Spirit instructed me, "Put those five smooth stones in the sling of praise and go conquer the enemy."

In this dramatic vision, God taught Fuchsia Pickett more about prayer and defeating the enemy of our souls than she had learned from her theological studies. Too often we have based our prayers on our ideas, our complaints, or our religious phrases to try to defeat the devil. Satan is not afraid of our religious formulas, our own thoughts, or our intellectual challenges. We must learn to use the effective spiritual weapons against him that God has given to us.

The *Word* of God washes us, sanctifies us, and renews our minds (see John 17:17; Rom. 12:1-2). The *blood* of Christ saves us from our sin and provides healing for us (see 1 Pet. 2:24; 1 John 1:7). When we are praying against principalities and powers in spiritual warfare with the enemy, we need to declare our covering in the blood of Jesus in that moment. We are doing very real battle against spirits without bodies and "spiritual wickedness in high places" (Eph. 6:12 KJV.)

The Scriptures teach that *faith* is a gift of God (see Eph. 2:8) and that it comes by hearing the Word of God (see Rom. 10:17). The apostle Paul declared: "The life which I now live in the flesh I live by the faith of the Son of God, who loved me and gave Himself for me" (Gal. 2:20b). And John declared, "This is the victory that overcometh the world, even our faith" (1 John 5:4b KJV). We need to learn to use this mighty weapon of faith and ask God to increase it.

We are also admonished in the Scriptures to be filled with the *Spirit* and to walk in the Spirit: "I say then: Walk in the Spirit, and you shall not fulfill the lust of the flesh" (Gal. 5:16). And Jesus taught us to ask in His *name* in order to receive what we need (see John 16:23-24).

As we allow our old wineskins to be renewed by the Word of God, we will learn to effectively use these spiritual weapons God has given us to defeat the enemy of our souls: His Word, His blood, His faith, His Spirit, and His name. Their supernatural power, when released through fervent prayer, will give to us the victory over the enemy of our souls that we so desperately need.

ENDNOTES

1. Archbishop Nicholas Duncan-Williams, www.actionworshipcenter.org.

2. Bishop Bart Pierce, Pastor, Rock City Church, Baltimore, MD., http://www.rockcitychurch.com.

3. Ibid.

4. Fuchsia Pickett, *Stones of Remembrance* (Lake Mary, FL: Charisma House, 1998), pp. 76-77.

CHAPTER 9

BREAKING THE SPEECH BARRIER

Power of Vocal Prayer

Because God's intention is for His Church to be a house of prayer, He expects prayer in the church to be a lifestyle, an occupation, a ministry, a continual release of supernatural power. One of the first barriers to be broken in order to establish the Church as His house of prayer is the *speech barrier*. Matthew Ashimolowo is the senior pastor of Kingsway International Christian Centre in London, England, a church of 8,000 members. He is author of over 30 books, including his wonderful book on prayer, *Breaking Barriers*.[1] Some of the concepts discussed here are drawn from the chapter he devotes entirely to the profound need of breaking the speech barrier in order to pray effectively.

It is clear from the Scriptures that men and women cried out to God vocally. And some of Jesus' prayers are recorded for us in the Gospels, showing that He also prayed aloud to His

Father. The enemy knows he has much to gain by keeping us quiet, so he has deceived many into striking a timid, reserved posture in prayer. Yet, it is difficult to overestimate the power of our words, for good or for evil.

We can never become authoritative in our praying until we learn to pray verbally the truth of God's Word. In the temptation of Jesus, He did not respond to the devil with railings of how awful the devil was to rebel against God in the first place. Jesus did not try to vex the devil by declaring His opinion of him. To overcome the temptation of the devil, Jesus simply declared: "It is written," followed by an applicable declaration from the Word of God (see Matt. 4). God has given us His written Word to use as a weapon against every onslaught of the enemy. In the same way Jesus did, we must release its power in our lives by speaking it out!

The Power of Verbal Expression

Our Creator has invested incredible power in verbal expression. In the Genesis account of creation, the Spirit was brooding over the earth, which was without form and void. And the creative power of God was released when *"God said, 'Let there be light'; and there was light"* (Gen. 1:3). The writer to the Hebrews describes Christ as "upholding all things by the word of His power" (Heb. 1:3). We have not understood the power of the spoken word, especially as it pertains to declaring the Word of God.

A student of revival for over three decades, I have been privileged to lead Holy Ghost breathed revivals in our church and in other nations. During these intense visitations of the Spirit of God, I have observed that when the Holy Spirit breaks in upon a people, they begin to speak freely. It becomes easy to repent, to pray, to exhort, to prophesy, to testify—all verbal expressions that may have been difficult for some before God stirred hearts in His manifest presence.

To overcome the temptation of the devil, Jesus simply declared: "It is written...."

Without the brooding of the Holy Spirit within us, we are uncomfortable in expressing our hearts in prayer. It is clear to me, as I have observed the presence of God release people into freedom of spiritual expression, that it is God's will and intention for believers to enjoy freedom of verbal declaration in prayer. The Word of God confirms His desire to give this freedom of expression. God spoke through His prophet, Hosea:

*O Israel, return to the Lord your God, for you have stumbled because of your iniquity; **take words with you**, and return to the Lord. Say to Him, "Take away all iniquity; receive us graciously, for we will offer the sacrifices of our lips"* (Hosea 14:1-2).

Amazingly, God responds to our words when we cry out to Him for His supernatural intervention. For example, when the angel, Gabriel, visited Daniel, he came in direct response to Daniel's prayer and fasting—his words were heard:

Do not fear, Daniel, for from the first day that you set your heart to understand, and to humble yourself before your God, your words were heard; and I have come **because of your words** (Daniel 10:12).

It is my experience that the people of God have to overcome a speech barrier in order to freely pray without any sense of self-consciousness or intimidation. I believe the restoration of praise and worship to the Church, which allows us to express our adoration to God freely, is   training us to release our voices in fervent, vocal prayer.

We Have a Verbal Gospel

From earliest times, the law of God has been spoken, memorized, chanted, sung, and maintained verbally when written language was simply the tedious task of a scribe. The roots of our Judeo-Christian heritage reveal a vocal gospel. There were not many available written copies of the Torah, so the children of Israel sang, chanted, and recited the Word of God. For example, Psalm 119 was written with first words of phrases following the Hebrew alphabet: Aleph, beth, gimel, daleth, he, waw, etc. This linguistic aid made it easier to memorize when reciting.

As we teach our children that "A" is for apple, Hebrew children were taught "Aleph" is for "Blessed are the undefiled in the way, who walk in the law of the Lord" (Ps. 119:1). By reciting the law of God, they were planting the divine seed of God in their hearts. The Old Testament command was for parents to focus their minds on the words God had given them, and then to give them to their children:

And these words which I command you today shall be in your heart. You shall teach them diligently to your children, and shall talk of them when you sit in your house, when you walk by the way, when you lie down, and when you rise up. You shall bind them as a sign on your hand, and they shall be as frontlets between your eyes. You shall write them on the doorposts of your house and on your gates (Deuteronomy 6:6-9).

Satan wants to keep God's people from making biblical declarations. He hates it when we say: "I am the righteousness of God in Christ"; "I am the healed of the Lord"; "I am blessed and highly favored." The devil trembles when we make biblical proclamation:

Now thanks be to God who always leads us in triumph in Christ (2 Corinthians 2:14).

For by You I can run against a troop, by my God I can leap over a wall (Psalm 18:29).

Oh, sing to the Lord a new song! For He has done marvelous things; His right hand and His holy arm have gained Him the victory (Psalm 98:1).

Jesus taught His disciples, "Most assuredly, I say to you, whatever you ask the Father in My name He will give you.... Ask, and you will receive, that your joy may be full" (John 16:23-24). As we release our requests of faith in simple words unto God, He hears and responds to our requests. We have only to break the speech barrier that satan uses to silence our tongues, knowing that our words have tremendous power in the presence of God.

THE SUPERNATURAL POWER OF WORDS

When God called Jeremiah to be a prophet, He touched His mouth and said:

Behold, I have put My words in your mouth. See, I have this day set you over the nations and over the kingdoms, to root out and to pull down, to destroy and to throw down, to build and to plant (Jeremiah 1:9-10).

---

*The devil trembles when
we make biblical proclamation.*

God was going to do radical things with His people, and He declared that His means of doing them was through the words He had put in Jeremiah's mouth. God's assignment for Jeremiah to change the nation of Israel required his declaring the word of the Lord, which would result in rooting out, pulling down, destroying, building, and planting. As the truth of God is preached, prayed, and otherwise declared, the Lord is *rooting out* things that are holding the Church back from His purposes. He is creating a clear path for His presence because He is getting ready to move mightily and swiftly, and He needs to have a people who are not fettered by tradition or personal agenda.

Through vocal prayer and spiritual warfare, we can *pull down* ruling principalities over lives, families, churches, and communities. Their evil purpose is canceled, and the will of God can be accomplished. For example, we need to declare the Word of God against the liberal mind-set influencing our nation, which wants to deny God in every sphere of life and destroy the very foundations of our Judeo-Christian heritage as a nation. We need to pull down the great strongholds of religious spirits and spirits of tradition, which have a "form of godliness" but deny its power.

We must determine to *destroy and throw down* the yokes of bondage over our personal lives. These bondages cause us to live in fear, unbelief, discouragement, unforgiveness, and sickness. We can enjoy the victory of Calvary as we plead the superior blood of Jesus over our bondages and declare the truths of God's Word in power. Then, we will see the seeds of revival truths *planted* into our lives and into the land. The purposes of God for His Church will be *built up*, giving us great hope for our nation turning to God.

When the religious leaders threatened the apostles and commanded them not to speak at all in the name of Jesus, Peter and John answered them, "*Whether it is right in the sight of God to listen to you more than to God, you judge. For we cannot but speak the things which we have seen and heard*" (Acts 4:19-20). Then the apostles went to church and reported what the religious leaders had said, and they began to pray. They asked God for boldness to speak the Word of God in the face of these threats. The Scriptures declare that they "raised their voice to God with one accord" (Acts 4:24), and such was the power of their prayer that "*the place where they were assembled together was shaken; and they were all filled with the Holy Spirit, and they spoke the word of God with boldness*" (Acts

4:31). The presence of God was manifest in power as the corporate cry went up to God as one voice.

It is difficult to overestimate the power of fervent, vocal cries to God to accomplish His purposes on the earth. We must allow our lives to become focused on the Kingdom of God, as these early Christians did, when they could not help but speak the things they had seen and heard. Even the established religious norms of the day, and threats from the religious authorities who denied the sacrifice of Christ, could not keep them from manifesting the power and glory of God in the earth.

Life and Death

King Solomon stated emphatically: *"Death and life are in the power of the tongue, and those who love it will eat its fruit"* (Prov. 18:21). He also understood that "you are snared by the words of your mouth; you are taken by the words of your mouth" (Prov. 6:2). His remedy for the snare of words was to "humble yourself" and go and "plead with your friend" to be released (Prov. 6:3).

Jesus Himself taught the overwhelming power of our words: *"For by your words you will be justified, and by your words you will be condemned"* (Matt. 12:37). And the apostle James taught that both blessing and cursing are pronounced by the unruly tongue (see James 3:8-10). He described the untamable tongue as a "fire, a world of iniquity" that has the power to defile the whole body and set "on fire the course of nature; and it is set on fire by hell" (James 3:6). While we value the freedom of speech as a constitutional right in this nation, do we realize the power of our words, for life or for death?

The prophet Isaiah referred to words as weapons: "No weapon formed against you shall prosper, and every tongue which rises against you in judgment you shall condemn" (Isa. 54:17). Even our youngest children have felt the sting of another child calling them names or speaking harshly to them. We have all experienced the destructive power of words when used as weapons against us. Yet, have we considered the "building" power of our words when declaring the Word of God in vocal prayer? There is supernatural power of life in God's Word to defeat every destructive, death-dealing force that emanates from the words of the evil one.

Believing an Evil Report

The nation of Israel failed to enter into the promised land because of the evil report the ten spies brought to the people (see Num. 13). The people chose to believe them instead of believing the words of the two spies, Caleb and Joshua, who brought back a good report. Caleb and Joshua declared the promises of God, knowing that because God was with them, they could defeat the enemies living in the promised land. Consequently, those two men were the only ones who lived to enter the promised land 40 years later. The others perished in the wilderness.

Years later, when the people of Israel had once again sinned against their God, He warned them through the prophet Jeremiah: "Return now every one from his evil way, and make your ways and your doings good" (Jer. 18:11b). But the people responded negatively, declaring: "That is hopeless! So we will walk according to our own plans, and we will every one obey the dictates [imagination] of his evil heart" (Jer. 18:12). Without Christ, the Bible declares that our imaginations are continually evil. When we come to Christ, we must allow the Holy Spirit to renew our minds with the truth, and choose to speak words of life.

If we do not discern between the good promises of God and the evil report, we will also perish. We must learn to cling to and confess the promises of God and disallow the negative projections all around us. We have to confront the negative imagination of our own mind and heart. Jesus said that "out of the abundance of the heart the mouth speaks" (Matt. 12:34). In order to speak positively, we must seek God to fill our hearts with His righteousness, peace, and joy in the Holy Ghost—which is His Kingdom (see Rom. 14:17).

How to Change Your Speech Patterns

Many people talk without really listening to what they are saying. They are not aware of the negative impact of their words or the complaining, bitter, harsh attitudes they reveal. The apostle James declared simply that "no man can tame the tongue" (James 3:8). For that reason, we are dependent upon the Holy Spirit working in our lives to change our speech patterns. As we allow Him to reveal the Word of God to us, and determine to fill our minds with the truth of the Scriptures, God Himself renews our minds and changes our attitude and expression.

We have to confront the negative imagination of our own mind and heart .

I encourage you to consider the following five steps to allowing the Holy Spirit to change your speech patterns:

1. **Begin to study the Word of God at your level of maturity in God.**

If you are a new Christian, study the Gospels and get acquainted with Jesus, your Savior. If you have been studying the Word for a while, go on to study the Epistles to learn what your Christian life should look like when growing toward maturity. Of course, everyone should read all of the Word, prayerfully, allowing the Holy Spirit to give you understanding.

2. **Fill your heart continually with the wonderful truths of God.**

Spending time with God is imperative. We cannot expect to speak the words of God if we are spending hours filling our minds with the speech of the world through TV, movies, music, and other sources. The psalmist declared: *"My heart is overflowing with a good theme; I recite my composition concerning the King; my tongue is the pen of a ready writer"* (Ps. 45:1). With his heart filled with the law of God, he was ready to extol the wonders of His King, as though his tongue were a pen, writing words of praise. What you put into your heart and mind will inevitably express itself.

3. **Speak the promises of the Word of God over your life.**

Learn to read a passage of Scripture that is filled with promise for believers and declare it personally over your life and situations. For example, declare in faith, *"The Lord is my shepherd, I shall not want. He makes me to lie down in green pastures; He leads me beside the still waters. He restores my soul; He leads me in the paths of righteousness for His name's sake"* (Ps. 23:1–3). Let the truth of God's promise of provision fill your heart. Don't give in to your fear of the negative circumstances you are facing. Confront your doubts with the promises of God, which are true.

4. Begin to decree God's Word prophetically.

Fill your mind with the Word until you can believe the promise of Jesus: *"For assuredly, I say to you, whoever says to this mountain, 'Be removed and be cast into the sea,' and does not doubt in his heart, but believes that those things he says will be done, he will have whatever he says"* (Mark 11:23). As we fill our hearts with the Word of God, faith grows and we can ask our heavenly Father for what we need and receive His bountiful provision.

5. Declare the creative Word of God.

Go for it! Begin to call things that are not as though they were. When God gave Abraham the promise of a son, it was humanly impossible because Sarah was past the age of child-bearing. The apostle Paul declares of Abraham, that he called those things which did "not exist as though they did" (Rom. 4:17). And their son, Isaac, was conceived. There is nothing too hard for God. He will accomplish His purposes in our lives as we dare to see them by faith and "call them as though they were."

As you dare to allow the Holy Spirit to change your speech patterns, you will come into a different realm of faith and prayer. You will begin to enter into the promise of Jesus that "whatever you bind on earth will be bound in heaven, and whatever you loose on earth will be loosed in heaven" (Matt. 18:18). The power and authority Jesus gives to those who will dare to speak His Word is truly awesome. We must activate that authority by speaking faith-filled words. We have to declare the truth of God regardless of circumstances or situations to the contrary. Bringing the truth of God's promises to bear in our lives depends on our speech patterns. The choice is ours to speak words of life or words of death.

ENDNOTE

1. Matthew Ashimolowo, *Breaking Barriers* (London: Matthew Ashimolowo Media Ministry, 2000).

CHAPTER 10

THE WAR OF WORDS

Proclaiming the Word of God

From our observation of the powerful prayer lives of our African friends, we learn that not only do they pray *vocally*, but their voices are also lifted in *proclamation of the Word of God* and His promises. They contend for the will of God as it is revealed in the Word of God. They declare that it will be manifest in their lives, their churches, and their nations. Following the example of Jesus, in His temptation in the wilderness, they declare to the enemy, "It is written" (see Matt. 4).

When we pray the Word,
we know we are praying the will of God.

The importance of keeping our praying centered on the Word of God cannot be over-emphasized. When we pray the Word, we know we are praying the will of God. Much of our praying has typically been traditional or sentimental. We learn rote prayers and recite them. Or we insert our feelings, desires, or opinions into our prayers. Because the Bible teaches that there are prayers that "avail much" (see James 5:16), we must conclude the possibility of prayers that do *not* avail much.

Too often we have prayed our preferences, our fears, our intellectual analysis. But the supernatural power of God will come into our praying only when we learn to consistently pray the Word of God. The Word of God is the promise of God, the will of God, the purpose of God. There is no mixture of fear and unbelief in our prayers when we simply declare the Word of God.

DAVID'S CONFIDENCE AGAINST GOLIATH

David's battle with Goliath is a great example of declaring faith in God. David displayed his strong confidence in the power of God when he challenged the giant, before whom all the army of Israel was cowering. In order to appreciate how the battle was really won, we need to consider the verbal confrontation between David and Goliath.

Goliath made a strong declaration against Israel: "I defy the armies of Israel this day; give me a man, that we may fight together" (1 Sam. 17:10). According to the Scriptures, his words greatly frightened Saul and all Israel (see 1 Sam. 17:11). The devil is still defying the people of God and too often the Church cowers before his threats. He continually defies the power of God, the people of God, and the purpose of God in the earth.

Where there is defiance against the living God, God Himself will raise up deliverers. It is up to faith-filled "Davids" to learn to confront the threats of the devil and to win in the name of the

Lord. We have to learn that the battle is not about us; it is about releasing the power of God that is in our hands. David's victory teaches us that God does not need great people, nor even great warriors; He needs weak people who trust in God's greatness.

David's brothers had no confidence in David, and neither did King Saul, who tried to give him his armor. David's confidence was not in himself. He declared to the king:

> *Your servant used to keep his father's sheep, and when a lion or a bear came and took a lamb out of the flock, I went out after it and struck it, and delivered the lamb from its mouth; and when it arose against me, I caught it by its beard, and struck and killed it. Your servant has killed both lion and bear; and this uncircumcised Philistine will be like one of them, seeing he has defied the armies of the living God...The Lord, who delivered me from the paw of the lion and from the paw of the bear, He will deliver me from the hand of this Philistine* (1 Samuel 17:34-37).

David was certain of the enemy's defeat because he had defied the armies of the living God. The reason we can expect satan's defeat in our situations is because he is defying the will of God. Jesus defeated the devil on the cross; it is up to us to enforce the victory of Calvary. Satan recognizes no authority but what we force him to recognize. For that reason Jesus said, "The kingdom of heaven suffers violence, and the violent take it by force" (Matt. 11:12). The Scriptures also declare, "If God is for us, who can be against us?" (Rom. 8:31b). We can be bold to take authority over the evil one because of our position in the Kingdom of God as believers.

David also rehearsed past victories in which he experienced the supernatural power of God to help him kill a lion and a bear. And he trusted the faithfulness of God to deliver this enemy of God into his hand in the same way. As we pray the Word of God, we are also rehearsing the victories of our God. We can rehearse personal victories as well, in which we have experienced the faithfulness of our God.

GOLIATH'S TAUNT

Goliath taunted David when he saw this youth coming out to fight him: "'Am I a dog, that you come to me with sticks?' And the Philistine cursed David by his gods. And the Philistine said to David, 'Come to me, and I will give your flesh to the birds of the air and the beasts of the field!'" (1 Sam. 17:43-44). This kind of venomous cursing and threatening can be scary. It's the kind of terrorizing speech that Saddam Hussein used when he said we were getting ready for "the mother of all wars."

These hate-filled threats from the enemy tend to stop us in our tracks. But what we learn from David is that we have to talk back to the devil. David stood his ground and declared what the real outcome of the battle would be. We are not going to win our battles against the enemy of our souls until we are ready to make declarations and proclamations according to the truth of God's Word. We need to focus on the *words* of David to discover the source of his faith:

David said to the Philistine, "You come against me with sword and spear and javelin, but I come against you in the name of the Lord Almighty, the God of the armies of Israel, whom you have defied" (1 Samuel 17:45 NIV).

David's confidence was not in his ability to use a slingshot, or in the smooth stone that he hurled at the giant. He knew that this giant was a representative of the enemies of God. Because they defied the living God, God would defeat them. David's words became a powerful weapon against the enemy, as he invoked the name of the living God. It is clear from the Scriptures that David understood that the battle against Goliath was spiritual. He declared to Goliath:

This day the Lord will deliver you into my hand, and I will strike you and take your head from you. And this day I will give the carcasses of the camp of the Philistines to the birds of the air and the wild beasts of the earth, that all the earth may know that there is a God in Israel. Then all this assembly shall know that the Lord does not save with sword and spear; for the battle is the Lord's, and He will give you into our hands (1 Samuel 17:46-47).

At that point, supernatural forces were summoned to fulfill the will of God. It took only one small stone hurled against the enemy, in faith in the name of God, to utterly defeat the entire army of the Philistines. What battle-hardened soldiers were unable to do because of fear, the word of the Lord in the mouth of a youth accomplished through faith.

We have to talk back to the devil.

Some people don't receive challenges from the devil because they are no threat to him. But some of us continually expose him, breaking the power of the strongman and taking more of his territory. We never stop praying, worshiping, warring, reaching out to deliver people that he holds in bondage. This infuriates the devil and he challenges our health, our calling, our finances, our very salvation. We must respond to the defiance of the devil against our lives by declaring the truth of God as David did.

Our own words won't defeat even a tiny demon. It is God's Word in our mouth that defeats the lies of the devil. Through David's verbal response he out-terrorized the terrorist; he "out-badded" the bad guy; he out-threatened the bully. David won the war of words against the accusing enemy, and then simply applied the natural means of the slingshot to seal the deal.

Believers have not always understood that the devil doesn't respond to anything but force. He doesn't respond to our human reasoning, our opinions, or even our desires. Remember the five weapons the Holy Spirit taught Fuchsia Pickett to use when she saw a vision of David fighting Goliath? They are: the name of God, the Word of God, the blood of Christ, the power of the Spirit, and our faith. Placed in the sling of praise, these powerful "stones" can be hurled at any enemy to vanquish him. David praised the God of Israel and declared that "the battle is the Lord's" (1 Sam. 17:47). He knew the victory was certain.

THE BREAD OF LIFE

Jesus continually taught in parables and used common metaphors of life to describe heavenly truths. For example, He taught: "I am the bread of life. ...I am the living bread which came down from heaven. If anyone eats of this bread, he will live forever; and the bread that I shall give is My flesh, which I shall give for the life of the world" (John 6:48,51). When the

Jews were offended and even His disciples did not understand His words, Jesus explained, "The words that I speak to you are spirit, and they are life" (John 6:63).

"The words that I speak to you are spirit, and they are life." —John 6:63

In the beginning of John's Gospel, he introduces Jesus as the Word: "In the beginning was the Word, and the Word was with God, and the Word was God. ...In Him was life, and the life was the light of men" (John 1:1,4). And when Jesus responded to the devil's temptation to make stones into bread, He declared, "It is written, Man shall not live by bread alone, but by every word that proceeds from the mouth of God" (Matt. 4:4). These metaphors point to the tangible way we experience the supernatural power of God in our lives. We eat the "Bread of Life"— by partaking of the Word of God, meditating on it, living by it. And we learn to live by "every word that proceeds from the mouth of God."

GETTING THE WORD IN—PRAYING IT OUT

There is a process for becoming an effective "pray-er" of the Word. This divine dynamic involves receiving the Word through reading, meditation, and divine revelation. Then the Word of God is released through your prayers. Sadhu Sundar Selvaraj gives us some wonderful clarity of the process of learning to pray effectively in the following steps.[1] Consider these steps in the process of getting the Word into your life and praying it out effectively, to receive the answers you need:

1. First of all, we must *cultivate a relationship with Jesus* by getting to know Him through the Word of God. As we read the Word daily, "eating the Bread of Life," we are sustained in our spiritual relationship with God. Without that relationship there will be no prayer life; and without prayer we cannot receive answers to our needs. Jesus promised: "If you remain in Me and My words remain in you, ask whatever you wish, and it will be given you (John 15:7 NIV).

2. Not only through reading the Word of God, but by *meditating* on it, allowing its truths to fill our thoughts, our spirits, will we grow in grace and increase in faith. God told Joshua, "This Book of the Law shall not depart from your mouth, but you shall meditate in it day and night, that you may observe to do according to all that is written in it. For then you will make your way prosperous, and then you will have good success" (Josh. 1:8).

3. As we become familiar with the will of God and the promises of God, we will be able to *pray the Word of God into our situations.* The Word will replace our ideas of how to pray, so that we can pray the will of God. The Holy Spirit will help us pray according to the will of God revealed in the Word. And the Scriptures promise that when we pray in the will of God, we have what we ask (see 1 John 3:22).

4. Even God's *prophetic promises must be prayed* in order to receive them into our lives. Daniel read in the books that the time of captivity for his people was over. Yet, they were still in captivity. So he set

himself to pray and fast, and God responded to his prayer. As a result, all of Heaven was activated and the promised deliverance came to pass. On another occasion, when God promised prophetically to restore Israel to her land, He said through the prophet Ezekiel, "I will also let the house of Israel inquire of Me to do this for them" (Ezek. 36:37).

5. When the apostle Paul described the *armor of God* that every believer is to wear, he showed us how to defeat the enemies' attacks. As part of our armor, we are to gird our waist with the truth and to take the sword of the Spirit, which is the Word of God, "praying always with all prayer and supplication in the Spirit" (Eph. 6:18).

6. The *Word of God is the substance of all prayer*, revealing the will of God for our lives, our families, our churches, and our nation. The Holy Spirit reveals to us the Word of God, and helps us to pray "according to the will of God" (Rom. 8:27).

7. Even the angels receive their assignments as they hear the Word of God. The psalmist declared: "Bless the Lord, you His angels, who excel in strength, who do His word, heeding the voice of His word" (Ps. 103:20). For God to send angelic powers to help us, we must learn to pray the Word of God.

When we understand that Jesus is the living Word, we realize why the battle raging against us is a *battle of words.* The battle of the ages is between the Word of God—Christ Jesus—and the defiant blasphemy of the evil one. Having the living Word in your heart and speaking the written Word is what satan greatly fears.

It is awesome to consider that when Christ returns, He is mounted on a white horse and His name is called "The Word of God" (Rev. 19:13). The Scriptures say that "out of His mouth goes a sharp sword, that with it He should strike the nations" (Rev. 19:15). The battle of words culminates in the ultimate victory of Christ, who wields the Word like a sharp sword going out of His mouth.

OVERCOMING IMPOSSIBLE SITUATIONS

When we keep our praying focused on the Word of God, declaring and proclaiming what He has promised, we are praying in the will of God. As we do, we shake the powers of darkness who fear, not us, but His Word in our mouths. Prayer in another dimension involves declaring and proclaiming the Word of God. We take a quantum leap of faith when we dare to believe God's Word in the face of impossible situations and declare it into the heavenlies. The patriarch, Job, understood the power of declaration for those who please God:

> ...then you will have your delight in the Almighty, and lift up your face to God. You will make your prayer to Him, He will hear you, and you will pay your vows. You will also declare a thing, and it will be established for you; so light will shine on your ways. When they cast you down, and you say, "Exaltation will come!" Then He will save the humble person. He will even deliver one who is not innocent; yes, he will be delivered by the purity of your hands (Job 22:26-30).

Situations that seem impossible are like mountains that must be removed by praying the Word of God. Remember that Jesus said we should speak to our mountain: "Have faith in God. For assuredly, I say to you, whoever says to this mountain, 'Be removed and be cast into the sea,' and does not doubt in his heart, but believes that those things he says will be done, he will have whatever he says" (Mark 11:22-23). Rather than talking about our problem or complaining about it, Jesus said we are to speak directly to it. When we speak we must believe that what we say will be done. We are to bring the will of God to bear on every difficulty, need, and problem and expect to receive supernatural victory.

We must realize that we are in a battle. According to the Scriptures, we have been called to "fight the good fight of faith" (1 Tim. 6:12). Of course, Jesus has already defeated satan on the cross. If that were not true, we could not hope to have victory over him. Our part is to *enforce* the victory of Calvary in our own lives. The fight of faith involves us in a war of words. Filling our hearts with the Word of God and declaring it in faith, we can defeat every giant that comes against the will of God for our destiny, our family, our church, and our nation.

ENDNOTE

1. Sadhu Sundar Selvaraj, retrieved from a cassette tape of Jesus Ministries, 2004 (205 DeAnza Blvd., Studio 91, San Mateo, CA 94402. Tel.: 650-349-7458. Fax: 650-349-7508).

CHAPTER 11

FERVENCY IN PRAYER

A Passionate Cry for God

During a particularly difficult season in my pastoral ministry, I felt oppressed—like I was a special target of the enemy's attacks. During that time, I had a recurring dream. In the dream I was a passenger in my own car, and the driver of the car would invariably drive me into a deep body of water. I would struggle to get out of the car and would then awaken from the dream. On one occasion, when I had this same dream, I managed to get out of the car and saw that I was in a river located in a deep canyon. I could see the steep cliffs on both sides of me rising up out of the river.

Then, when I looked to one side of the canyon, I saw Jesus. My eyes were fixed on Him, and I was astonished at what I saw. Jesus had chains wrapped around Him and He was on His knees. His hair was disheveled and His face was dusty, as if He were a common laborer. Tears ran down His cheeks and left streaky trails in the dust. As I stood transfixed watching Him, I began to argue theology in my dream. I thought, *satan is bound; Jesus is not supposed to be bound in chains.*

But as I looked into His eyes, I could see the great compassion and determination He felt for me. That look screamed to me, "I will make a way for you." Though this vision occurred over 20 years ago, when I think of it, I can still see His eyes, and I weep. Suddenly, He looked up to Heaven, and I heard Him cry, "O God, in the name of God." Again, I did not understand the scriptural basis for praying "in the name of God." My mind faltered for a moment in its theological query. But, instantly, when Jesus cried out, His chains fell off. He leaped from one side of that deep canyon to the other—and I was free.

I awakened immediately and jumped out of bed. The Holy Spirit spoke to me, "Read John chapter 17." I went to my Bible and read Jesus' prayer for His disciples: "Holy Father, keep through *Your name* those whom You have given Me, that they may be one as We are. While I was with them in the world, I kept them in *Your name*" (John 17:11b-12). That was the first time I realized that Jesus used the name of God as the keeping power for those who follow Him. His fervent passion impacted me and continues to impact me to this day.

"O God, in the name of God!"

Then the Holy Spirit impressed my spirit in a new way with the verse: "For we have not an high priest who cannot be touched with the feeling of our infirmities" (Heb. 4:15a KJV). I understood His chains in the vision to be His "feeling" the bondage of my infirmity, the oppression I was experiencing at that time in my life. I never had that recurring dream again.

From the moment I awakened from my vision of Jesus, the oppression in my mind was gone; I was completely healed. God had released me from the oppression of the enemy through His power revealed to me in a spiritual dream.

The impact of Jesus' fervent, vocal cry to God left a deep impression on me. It gave me a deeper understanding of the reality of the Scripture:

> *Therefore He is also able to save to the uttermost those who come to God through Him, since He always lives to make intercession for them* (Hebrews 7:25).

How can we ever fathom the love of our Savior, who is, even now, at the right hand of the Father in Heaven, praying fervently for each one of us to be "saved to the uttermost"? I heard the testimony of an Indian evangelist to Nepal who had an extraordinary experience with Jesus. Sadhu Sundar Selvaraj had retired to his room to pray specifically for the 300 people who were supporting his evangelistic ministry in the nation of Nepal. When he set himself to seek God, he always told people that he was not to be disturbed, not even by his mother. So, on this occasion, when he had begun to pray and heard a knock on his door, he was frustrated that his request was not being honored.

He went to the door and flung it open, ready to react to his intruder. But when the door opened, he recognized Jesus standing there. Overwhelmed, Selvaraj heard Jesus say, "I have come to pray with you." Selvaraj invited Him into the room, closed the door, and knelt down again to pray. Jesus knelt with him. Selvaraj felt that he shouldn't be watching, but it was impossible to take his eyes off his heavenly Visitor. He saw Jesus kneel down and begin to weep, naming aloud every one of the 300 believers who were supporting Selvaraj's ministry. He saw Jesus' shoulders shake as He wept over these precious believers. Selvaraj was deeply moved by the tenderness of Jesus as He prayed fervently that day.[1]

How we have missed the intimate relationship of love with our Savior when we fail to set aside time to pray. We haven't realized how He longs to be with us and to help us in every situation. It is in communion with Him alone that our deepest needs are met. God is love and we can drink deeply of that love only as we spend time in His presence.

MISCONCEPTION OF PRAYER

One great misconception about prayer is that there is no effort involved. We sometimes treat prayer as a passionless business arrangement, coming to God to mumble our petitions. Then we sit back and wait for Him to "lay it on us." The devil may also suggest to us that prayer should never make us tired. In our "microwavable" society, the devil deceives Christians into thinking we can just casually address the throne of God and expect to receive the answer to our prayers. This is not the biblical pattern for receiving the promises of God.

The Scriptures depict prayer as a strenuous activity. For example, the psalmist declared: "Pour out your heart before Him; God is a refuge for us" (Ps. 62:8b). And the New Testament refers to "laboring fervently...in prayers" (Col. 4:12). While we do not consider it strange or out of order to work hard at our job, our sport, recreation, or hobby, many Christians avoid exerting effort when it comes to prayer. God responds to strength of desire and heartfelt expression of that desire.

When Hannah prayed year after year that the Lord would take her barrenness and give her a son, the Scriptures record her anguish of heart. She went into the temple to pray, and so intense was her cry that she could not even speak; only her lips moved in prayer. Eli the priest watched her and concluded that she was drunk. But Hannah replied, "No, my lord, I am a woman of sorrowful spirit. I have drunk neither wine nor intoxicating drink, but have poured out my soul before the Lord...out of the abundance of my complaint and grief I have spoken until now" (1 Sam. 1:15-16).

The Scriptures depict prayer as a strenuous activity.

Eli pronounced a blessing over her and proclaimed that the God of Israel would grant her petition (see 1 Sam. 1:17). The simple declaration of that blessing took the sadness from Hannah's countenance. God answered her fervent prayer and gave her the blessing of conceiving a son, whom she called Samuel. She fulfilled her vow in offering him to the Lord. Then she bore other children to her husband as God continued to bless her womb.

Even the Old Testament pattern of prayer that was heard and answered by God involved deep longing and pouring out of the soul to Him. These saints understood that if they cried unto God, He would hear and respond to them. They did not live under the misconception that prayer was a "moment of silence" or a casual speaking of words on the run. They set themselves to seek God in order to receive miracles from His hand.

GOD'S WILL—OR MINE?

We have discussed our need to be vocal in prayer. However, unless our words are filled with fervent desire—passion—for God's will, they will be unfruitful. We have to take stock of our own desires, goals, and ambitions to see if we really desire the will of God for our lives. It is God's will that we walk in destiny, fulfilling His divine purposes. And it is God's desire that all people be saved from eternal damnation. He wants to use us in His grand design to win the lost. Until we abandon ourselves to God, praying sincerely, "Thy kingdom come, Thy will be done in earth, as it is in heaven" (Matt. 6:10 KJV), we will lack passion and fervency in prayer. Our selfish requests will not bring us the fulfillment we seek. And God cannot give us anything less than His will for our lives.

The Scripture declares plainly that the "kingdom of heaven suffers violence, and the violent take it by force" (Matt. 11:12). The word translated "violence" is *biazo*, which means "to force or crowd oneself into, to press" (Strong's #971). When Jesus taught that the gate to destruction is broad and spacious, He declared: "But the gate is narrow (contracted by pressure) and the way is straitened and compressed that leads away to life, and few are those who find it" (Matt. 7:14 AMP).

Violence, pressure, force—these are words filled with the energy of passion to "get what you want." If you want your own way, you will find a broad road—that leads to destruction. But if you truly desire God's will, you will have to endure pressure, perhaps from your peers, your family, and even your own "self-life." Unselfish prayer is that which makes you become one with the will of God, feeling His heart of compassion. Zeal for righteousness, peace, and joy in the Holy Spirit reflects the Kingdom of God in the earth (see Rom. 14:17).

LABORING FERVENTLY IN PRAYER

Prayer is not a free ride; it is hard work. It is the "effectual *fervent* prayer" that avails much (James 5:16 KJV). The Scriptures use strong words like labor, wrestling, agonizing, and travail to describe prayer. These are words of passion. Passion is the energy of emotion—fervency—that gives strength to concern and desire. Intellectual prayers that lack passion will be unfruitful. We must experience the strength of desire that only the Holy Spirit can give to make us passionately fervent in prayer.

Prayer is not a free ride; it is hard work.

Consider the pattern of Jesus' prayers as described by the Scriptures: "Who, in the days of His flesh, when He had offered up prayers and supplications, with vehement cries and tears to Him who was able to save Him from death, and was heard because of His godly fear, though He was a Son, yet He learned obedience by the things which He suffered" (Heb. 5:7-8). We know that in the Garden of Gethsemane Jesus, "being in agony, He prayed more earnestly. Then His sweat became like great drops of blood falling down to the ground" (Luke 22:44).

So great was the exertion and fervor of His travail, that God the Father sent an angel from Heaven who appeared to Jesus and strengthened Him (see Luke 22:43). The prophet Isaiah had foreseen this agony, when he declared: "He shall see of the travail of His soul, and shall be satisfied" (Isa. 53:11 KJV). Christ was travailing in prayer to bring many sons into the Kingdom of God. His strength of desire reflects the Father's heart that is "not willing that any should perish but that all should come to repentance" (2 Pet. 3:9).

OVERCOMING OUR FLESH

The disciples did not share Jesus' burden that night; they were overcome by grief and simply went to sleep. Unable to bear the magnitude of Christ's travail, they were not able to watch even one hour with Him. Jesus simply commented: "The spirit indeed is willing, but the flesh is weak" (Matt. 26:41b). But He also warned them to "watch and pray, *lest you enter into temptation*" (Matt. 26:41a).

The disciples' grief was centered on how Jesus' impending death made them feel, their fears, dreads, and the impact of the loss of their Lord on their own psyches—their future. Sleeping was a "cop-out" for facing the reality of God's purposes, which they could not understand. They were intimidated by the fervor and intensity of Jesus' agony, His strong crying. It filled them with a sense of impending doom. So they slept.

Fervent prayer requires death to our self-life.

As believers, we can overwhelmingly relate to the "weakness" of these disciples. When we are facing difficult situations, we say things like, "I can't cope with this," or "Why is God allowing this in my life?" If our situation hurts, if it is uncomfortable, inconvenient, if it stretches us, we try to "avoid" it. We may try to make excuses or even criticize people around our problem. We wonder what people will think, how we will look in the eyes of others. The enemy uses our reactions to keep us from fervent, powerful prayer in the face of difficulty. Fervent prayer requires a death to all our self-life, filled with its emotional reactions, its intellectual reasoning, and selfish choices for our comfort and ease.

MODERN MARTYRS FOR CHRIST

In nations like China, Christians know nothing of comfort or convenience. Millions of Christians worship in secret house churches where they pray fervent prayers for the saints and receive ministry of the Word. All who attend these underground churches are considered criminals against the state. Their plight with the government is so difficult that they expect to spend years in prison when discovered and to be brutally tortured for their faith. Most do not expect to live a long life; many are martyred for their faith.[2]

Brother Yun, known to Chinese Christians as the "Heavenly Man," has been used mightily by God to develop the underground church in China. He is a wanted criminal and has been arrested and tortured many times. He has spent many years in prison, and escaped miraculously from the tightest security prison in China. During one intense time of torture, he cried out to God that He would "receive his spirit." He writes of his experience:

On my way to prison, the guards traveling in the back of the van switched on an electric baton when they heard me praying and jolted me with shocks. The pain was too severe for me and I felt my heart and my brain were going to literally explode from my body. I cried to the Lord, "God, have mercy on me. Please receive my spirit now." The word of the Lord came to me clearly, "The reason you suffer is so you can partake in the fellowship of My suffering. Be still and know that I am God. I will be exalted among the nations. I will be exalted in the earth." In my proud heart I'd been thinking that I was important to the church, that they needed me to lead them. Now, I vividly understood that He is God and I am but a feeble man. I realized...that if He ever chose to use me again it would be nothing more than a great privilege. Suddenly the fear and pain left me.[3]

These valiant Christians have proven the adage, "Calamity clarifies." They know what they are about and they pursue it with strength, zeal, and commitment. In their no-nonsense system of underground churches in China, their credentials are not recognized by theological degrees. Rather, their ministry is validated by the power of God working through them, the number of times they have been arrested, the years spent in prison, the torture they have survived. They understand what it is to love their enemies and have won many of them to Christ. Economically, these persecuted Christians have so little that they "tithe" their lives. It is common for newly converted Christians to give the first seven years of their lives in service as a tithe to God.

"BUT I HAVE RAISED UP 300 CHURCHES"

My friend, Ralph Mahoney, founder of World Map, told me this wonderful story of the power of fervent, selfless prayer. He said that he and some other American ministers had created a training manual for pastors of churches to be used only in nations outside the United States. They offered the manual to Chinese pastors for the purpose of establishing the house churches they had planted. When a little woman learned of this offer, she came to Ralph Mahoney and asked him for 300 manuals. In amazement he replied, "I'm sorry, I can only give you one manual for each house church, not for each person in your church." Her startling response was, "But I have raised up 300 churches."

"But I have raised up 300 churches."

You can imagine Ralph's astonishment as he asked her, "Would you tell me how you did that?" Her story was simple. Having dedicated the first seven years of her converted life to serve Jesus alone, she asked a farmer in a nearby village if he would be willing for her to work for him and sleep in his field at night, allowing her to glean from the crop that was left in the field. He agreed, and she began her prayer vigil for the people of that village. Before long a family asked her to stay in their little tenant shack. Soon, she led a family member to faith in Jesus.

This new convert soon led other family members to faith in Christ. They experienced the peace of God that salvation through Christ brings. Together they began to share their faith with others in the village. They prayed for them to receive Christ, and began to receive His blessings of divine protection and provision for their lives. It was not long until the little woman had a church of 45 new believers.

Then she moved to the next village and repeated the process. At the end of seven years of dedicating her life solely to prayer and service, she had established 300 house churches, which of course, are considered illegal criminal organizations to the Chinese government! In these house churches, miracles happen on a regular basis. The story of this pastor could be multiplied many times. In the nation of China today, so many new converts are being won to Christ daily that no one wants to put a number on it for fear of reprisal by the government.

The Holy Spirit will empower us to win souls in our culture as we seek to do the will of God. He will empower us to pray and break strongholds that bind people from the truth as we submit our lives to fervent prayer.

ENDNOTES

1   Sadhu Sundar Selvaraj testimony, retrieved from a cassette tape of Jesus Ministries, 2004 (205 DeAnza Blvd., Studio 91, San Mateo, CA 94402. Tel.: 650-349-7458. Fax: 650-349-7508).

2. Brother Yun with Paul Hattaway, *The Heavenly Man* (London & Grand Rapids, MI: Monarch Books, 2002).

3. Ibid., p. 92.

CHAPTER 12

FERVENCY EXPRESSED

Birthing Through Travail

The Scriptures clearly indicate that even the prophetic promises of God must be prayed through in order to be fulfilled. As Pastor Augustine taught us, "Prophecy must be birthed in the womb of prayer." The apostle James declares that the "effective, fervent prayer of a righteous man avails much" (James 5:16). He refers to the prophet Elijah's prayer for rain, declaring that he prayed earnestly that it would rain at the end of the famine, and it did (see James 5:17-18).

It is important to note that Elijah travailed to bring forth the rain that God had *already promised* to send. It was not enough to hear God's promise; the prophet understood his responsibility was to pray until the promise could be manifest. Elijah did not have a "minute of silent prayer" to ask God for rain. He didn't throw up a casual, "OK, God, do what You promised to do." When Elijah sought God for rain, according to the Scriptures, he took the Hebrew woman's position of birthing and travail: "And Elijah went up to the top of Carmel; then he bowed down on the ground, and put his face between his knees" (1 Kings 18:42). He sent his servant out seven times to look at the sky for evidence that his prayer was being answered. Not until he saw a cloud the size of a man's hand did Elijah cease praying. Then he declared that his prayers were answered and went into action.

The New Testament commentary on Elijah's travail declares that "Elijah was a man with a nature like ours, and he prayed earnestly that it would not rain; and it did not rain on the land for three years and six months. And he prayed again, and the heaven gave rain, and the earth produced its fruit" (James 5:17-18). It was the prophet's travail that brought fulfillment of the prophetic word of the Lord for a nation. It was his fervent prayer that caused fire to descend from Heaven to consume the sacrifice in his challenge to the prophets of Baal.

The spirit of Elijah is a spirit of travail
to bring forth the purposes of God.

The process for birthing the promises of God through travail is clearly taught in the Scriptures. God places a seed of understanding in our hearts for His purposes in our life, our church, or our nation. It is a seed of destiny with which He "impregnates" us in order to fulfill His purposes in the earth. There is a season of waiting and nurturing of that seed, and then when it is time to bring it to birth, we have to "push" in prayer to bring the new life forth. This "push time" is painful; it is not comfortable to labor and travail in prayer to bring forth the new life God has promised. But if that new life is not birthed in a timely way, there will be serious consequences.

In the natural, when a woman has complications in giving birth, doctors resort to surgical means to save the life of the newborn. Cesarean birth requires major surgery, a cutting of the flesh. In the spiritual realm, this cutting away is an analogy for a cutting of our flesh life. God may allow emotional oppression, relational problems, financial difficulties, or other attacks of the enemy to "cut your flesh" in order to protect the life of the "newborn"—the purpose and destiny of God for your life. He does not want to abort His will for your life through an inability to bring it forth. He will use drastic means to bring you to preserve the divine life and destiny He has placed within you.

The spirit of Elijah is a spirit of travail to bring forth the purposes of God. God is calling a people today who will birth His purposes in the earth through travailing prayer. He promised to send the spirit of Elijah before the "great and dreadful day of the Lord" (Mal. 4:5). God spoke through His prophet Malachi this wonderful promise:

> *Behold, I will send you Elijah the prophet before the coming of the great and dreadful day of the Lord. And he will turn the hearts of the fathers to the children, and the hearts of the children to their fathers, lest I come and strike the earth with a curse* (Malachi 4:5-6).

The New Testament records the fulfillment of this promise with the coming of John the Baptist:

> *He will also go before Him in the spirit and power of Elijah, "to turn the hearts of the fathers to the children," and the disobedient to the wisdom of the just, to make ready a people prepared for the Lord* (Luke 1:17).

This prophetic promise of John the Baptist's birth came to the aged Zecharias in the place of prayer. As Zecharias simply went into the temple to pray, to fulfill his obedience as a priest of God, an angelic visitation shocked him with the promise of a miracle. His wife Elizabeth, barren into her old age, would conceive and bear a son. When John the Baptist grew up he came as the "voice of one crying in the wilderness: 'Prepare the way of the Lord'" (Luke 3:4). He cried out in fervent passion to prepare the way of the Lord, to bring fulfillment of the purposes of God in the earth. He made disciples, baptizing them and teaching them to pray.

When Jesus' disciples asked Him to teach them to pray, one of them said, "Lord, teach us to pray, *as John also taught his disciples*" (Luke 11:1). The spirit of Elijah resting on John the Baptist was a spirit of prayer. It was the same spirit that consumed Elijah when he prayed to the God of Heaven to send fire on his sacrifice in his battle against the false god of Baal and then again when he prayed for rain. We have lost the essence of the power of these prophets when we relegate prayer to "saying grace" over our food or "mentioning" our loved ones in prayer. These Bible heroes were consumed with birthing the purposes of God.

One of the saddest laments in the Bible is when God spoke to Ezekiel: "I sought for a man among them who would make a wall, and stand in the gap before Me on behalf of the land, that I should not destroy it; but I found no one" (Ezek. 22:30). The prayers of an intercessor could have held back God's judgment that was ready to be poured out upon a wicked nation; but there was none.

It is astounding that God can be called upon to withhold judgment because of the prayers of believers. We have the privilege and responsibility to seek God for mercy on our nation in order that we may see many come to repentance and turn to Christ. That will involve travail and fervent prayer—in another dimension. If the Church does not stand in the gap in prayer, God has no choice but to pour out His judgment.

The prayers of an intercessor could have held back God's judgment.

"As Soon as Zion Travailed..."

The prophet Isaiah records these poignant questions regarding birthing the purposes of God:

> *Who hath heard such a thing? Who hath seen such things? Shall the earth be made to bring forth in one day? Or shall a nation be born at once? For as soon as Zion travailed, she brought forth her children. Shall I bring to the birth, and not cause to bring forth? saith the Lord: Shall I cause to bring forth, and shut the womb? saith thy God* (Isaiah 66:8-9 KJV).

God promises to bring forth new life as Zion—the Church—travails. Throughout the New Testament, this principle of travail is taught as well. The apostle Paul calls the Galatians his little children "for whom I labor in birth again until Christ is formed in you" (Gal. 4:19). These Christians were not established in the spiritual realities of faith in Christ alone. Paul wrote to them showing them their error. While his letter was intended to set them straight doctrinally, he knew the key to their conversion was to travail in prayer until Christ was formed in them. True spiritual life must be birthed in the womb of travailing prayer.

CONTENDING FOR THE PRIZE

The apostle Paul described Epaphras as "a bondservant of Christ...always laboring fervently for you in prayers, that you may stand perfect and complete in all the will of God" (Col. 4:12). "Laboring fervently" is translated from the Greek *agonizomai*, which literally means "to compete for a prize" (Strong's #75). It involves contending with an adversary, striving and fighting. Fervent prayer strives against forces of darkness that keep the Kingdom of God from being manifest in the earth.

Sometimes our lack of intensity and fervency in prayer may be due to apathy or sheer laziness. It may also be simple ignorance of the biblical pattern for prayer. As I have mentioned, it is a biblical principle that the promises and prophetic plans of God must be brought into manifestation through the womb of prayer. They must be birthed through the travail that is willing to press into the purposes of God until....

Fervent prayer strives against forces of darkness.

God's agenda in the earth to give us His Kingdom of righteousness, peace, and joy in the Holy Ghost must be fulfilled in human vessels. There is no other way to bring the Kingdom of God to earth. Through prayer we activate the heavens into accomplishing God's purposes on the earth. We see that reality manifested in the life of Daniel and Elijah, who prayed earnestly and received the wonderful manifestation of answers to their prayers. Only fervent prayer will birth God's purposes!

RECEIVING THE PROMISE

I love the story of Anna, the prophetess who received the promised Messiah in His infancy. It is a brief account of a very long and dedicated life to prayer for the coming Messiah. Yet it is filled with the wonderful reality of the power of travailing prayer to bring to birth His purposes in the earth:

> *Now there was one, Anna, a prophetess, the daughter of Phanuel, of the tribe of Asher. She was of a great age, and had lived with a husband seven years from her virginity; and this woman was a widow of about eighty-four years, who did not depart from the temple, but served God with fastings and prayers night and day. And coming in that instant she gave thanks to the Lord, and spoke of Him to all those who looked for redemption in Jerusalem* (Luke 2:36-38).

Anna's brief mention in the Scriptures is very significant in its revelation of the value God places on making prayer a way of life. She is honored to be among the first to receive the newborn Messiah, and to make Him known throughout Jerusalem. Her joy reflects the joy of Heaven in giving the Savior to mankind. Our lives can be filled with supernatural joy in the face of rigorous circumstances of life as we yield our lives to become a part of birthing the purposes of God through prayer.

The apostle Paul also exhorts regarding prayer: "…that supplications, prayers, intercessions, and giving of thanks be made for all men, for kings and all who are in authority, that we may lead a quiet and peaceable life in all godliness and reverence" (1 Tim. 2:1-2). Paul understands that fervent prayer is the key to living a godly life. He teaches that as we pray we can change our communities and our nations, in order to live in peace. Receiving the promises of God for every situation in life requires that we dedicate our entire lives to all kinds of prayer.

Paul understands that fervent prayer is the key to living a godly life.

CHAPTER 13

FOCUSING ON GOD ALONE

A Vertical Perspective

During the African prayer summits in which I have participated, hosted by my African mentors, I witnessed that every person there was praying aloud with intensity and fervency. Their entire concentration was *vertical*, that is, their focused attention was uplifted to God alone. One person led in prayer for specific needs and the others expressed their agreement. During this corporate prayer service, no one in the meeting was sitting (unless there was a physical difficulty).

Everyone was standing, walking, lifting their hands, and sometimes clapping. They began to make biblical declarations and proclamations concerning the Kingdom of God, praying for specific promises of God to be manifest among them. They declared the Word of God in prayer boldly, with authority and faith.

It is not surprising that after declaring the promises of the Word of God and proclaiming liberty to the captives, miracles begin to happen in their midst. They begin to move into the prophetic realm of prayer. Supernatural faith comes into their hearts as they proclaim the Word. Their praying takes on a heavenly perspective, seeing all of life from God's viewpoint, rather than man's. Their vocal agreement with the spiritual realities they are declaring raises the faith level in the entire congregation.

Another observation I made from participating in these African prayer summits is that these praying Christians are apparently not intimidated by other people. Their prayers are focused *vertically*, addressing the throne of God. They are not bound by fear of men's faces. These believers are not concerned about anyone's opinions of their prayers. This single-eyed focus on God alone also reflects the New Testament pattern of corporate prayer:

> *And when they heard that, they lifted up their voice to God with one accord, and said, Lord, Thou art God, which hast made heaven, and earth, and the sea, and all that in them is, who by the mouth of thy servant David hast said, Why did the heathen rage, and the people imagine vain things?* (Acts 4:24-25 KJV)

Even as the religious rulers of the day threatened the apostles, the Church gathered to pray together and make proclamation from the Word of God. So fervent was their prayer and so effective, that the Scriptures declare, "When they had prayed, the place was shaken where they were assembled together; and they were all filled with the Holy Ghost, and they spake the word of God with boldness" (Acts 4:31 KJV).

In Dr. Cho's church, when thousands of believers pray together in the sanctuary, their voices sound like the roar of a rushing waterfall. Yet, when a little bell is rung, everyone immediately stops praying. Such fervent sound of thousands of voices raised in prayer together does not reflect disorder, as some would conclude. Rather, it reflects the biblical order of focused prayer, lifting voices together in abandon to call on God.

---

*Their prayers have one focus, which is **vertical**.*

Of course, this biblical pattern of prayer does not fit the "religious order" of churches where prayers are "led" by one unemotional clergyman, intoning God's will, while the congregation sits in silence as spectators. Perhaps you could argue that there is room for cultural differences in our approach to prayer. However, I believe there is more involved in our sense of "order" than a difference in cultural style. The African church has entered into a divine focus on God according to the biblical pattern, which gets God's attention. Their prayer is expressed in a fervent, passionate, seeking of God with their whole heart. Such fervency cannot be expressed through staid, conventional prayers, and much less through tacit agreement.

As I have been teaching these principles in our church, as well as other churches where I minister, I have observed that old habits are hard to break. It is difficult to give up the "spectator" mentality, sitting quietly while someone else calls on God. It is contrary to the tradition of many to pray fervently and vocally in "public." I believe these are religious paradigms, which relate to the metaphor of "old wineskins." We need to return to the biblical pattern of corporate prayer. Preaching, worship, and working for God are powerless and purposeless unless they are birthed in the womb of fervent prayer.

THE BIBLICAL PATTERN

The psalmist declared: "I cried to the Lord with my voice, and He heard me from His holy hill" (Ps. 3:4). In the Hebrew, the word David used for "cried" is *qará*, which we have noted means to call out, to encounter, to accost a person (Strong's #7121). There is a definite interaction with the one to whom you "*qará.*" That imperative call requires a divine response. David declared that God heard his cry—he encountered God and God responded.

Of course, having freedom to cry out to God involves more than learning to give vocal expression to prayer. Sometimes there is a spiritual bondage in our hearts and minds that must be broken in order for us to be able to focus on God alone. The enemy does not want God's people to be free. He cringes when he hears bold, authoritative prayers. And when we are free to pray God's Word with power and authority, satan knows that we have laid hold on a mighty weapon that pulls down his strongholds.

When God called Jeremiah to be His prophet, He placed His words in Jeremiah's mouth, and declared: "You shall go to all to whom I send you, and whatever I command you, you shall speak" (Jer. 1:7b). Then God immediately issued this solemn warning: "Do not be dismayed before their faces, lest I dismay you before them" (Jer. 1:17b). God warned Jeremiah against the fear of men, promising to be with him and fight for him. Yet, if he gave in to the fear of man, he would pay the consequences.

Freedom to call upon God without considering what others think or wondering how we sound is not optional—it is imperative. In order for God's blessing and victory to be ours, we must seek the freedom to call on God. Our focus must be vertical, not horizontal, for fervent, faith-filled prayer to bring the desired results.

AT EASE IN ZION

Through the prophet Amos, God pronounced woe on those who trusted in the safety and power of their city. To those who were content with the state of things and reveled in their riches God declared:

Woe to you who are at ease in Zion, and trust in Mount Samaria, notable persons in the chief nation, to whom the house of Israel comes! (Amos 6:1)

"Woe to you who are at ease in Zion."—Amos 6:1

Bible commentators explain that God's people in those days living within the safety of Zion's strong fortress were enjoying soft, comfortable lives, given to sensuality. They believed that, by virtue of association, they were exempt from divine judgment. They felt secure in their own power and the strong security of the walls of Zion around them. They also looked to the strength of their neighboring kingdom, Samaria, for security. God pronounced woe upon them for placing their trust in something less than Himself. They had become great among the kingdoms of the earth, and in their greatness, had fallen prey to pride in their own strength. Theirs was a false security, which evoked a "woe" from God. "This woe applies to the great men in Zion and Samaria, that is to say, to the chiefs of the whole of the covenant nation, because they were all sunk in the same godless security."[1]

Of course, Zion is a biblical type of the Church, the Body of Christ in the earth. While the church is to be a strong, safe place for believers, its biblical purpose is to be a dwelling place for the presence of God—a house of prayer for all nations. And the Church, which is the Body of Christ in the earth, under the Lordship of Christ, is meant to fulfill the Great Commission that Jesus gave the disciples. The same love and compassion Jesus displayed when He walked the earth is meant to fill our hearts as believers.

As we place our trust in Christ, our Redeemer, we desire to reach out to lost and hurting humanity, offering them the security and safety of life in God. The more we surrender our lives to prayer, the more God's heart for lost humanity will fill our desires. We will be motivated and empowered to fulfill the Great Commission.

False Security

Yet, there are many Christians who unwittingly place their trust in the church itself to save them—by association. They suffer from a false sense of security. They feel that if they fulfill a set of prescribed religious traditions they are safe from the judgments of God, though they are not cultivating personal relationship with Him. They are not focused on the purposes of God for the salvation of souls. They live for their own pleasure, which they believe is sanctioned by the church. And they become proud in the status they have in the Christian community.

Without a godly focus on God and His purposes, they lack concern for their neighbors, lack compassion for the lost, and live utterly self-centered lives. In short, they are "at ease in Zion."

Another translation of "at ease in Zion" renders it to mean "complacent" (Amos 6:1 NIV). Many of the woes being experienced by the church today are due to ungodly complacency. Focus on the American dream and an affluent lifestyle has blinded hearts of believers to the real mission of the Church. It is apparent that we are living in the last days. The apostle Paul described the last days as "perilous times," when people would trust in a "form of godliness" but deny its power:

In the last days perilous times will come: For men will be lovers of themselves, lovers of money, boasters, proud, blasphemers, disobedient to parents, unthankful, unholy, unloving, unforgiving, slanderers, without self-control, brutal, despisers of good, traitors, headstrong, haughty, lovers of pleasure rather than lovers of God, **having a form of godliness but denying its power** *(2 Timothy 3:1-5).*

The prophet, Isaiah, also lamented: "All our righteousnesses are like filthy rags; we all fade as a leaf, and our iniquities, like the wind, have taken us away. And there is no one who calls on Your name, who stirs himself up to take hold of You" (Isa. 64:6b-7). He made it clear that it is our responsibility to stir ourselves up and to call on God. We must take hold of God and stretch ourselves in prayer until we know that He has heard and answered us.

There is a paradigm, a "spiritual culture," in our nation that is unaware of the necessity to fervently seek God *until....* In the early Pentecostal movement at the turn of the 20th century, Christians referred to fervent prayer as "praying through." They understood the strength of intercession that birthed the promises of God. Their hearts were focused on manifesting God's power in the earth, resulting in transformed lives, miraculous healings, and powerful protection and deliverance from the enemy of our souls.

In contrast, many in the American church today have become "at ease in Zion," placing confidence and trust in our affluence, our intellectual prowess, and our church programs. Our culture values ease and comfort, convenience and pleasure—all watchwords for success. Much of this ungodly mentality has been incorporated into the way we "do church." Some churches advertise "casual dress, come as you are"—be comfortable.

Our culture values ease and comfort.

While there is nothing intrinsically wrong with dressing comfortably, the mind-set of pursuing personal comfort does not equate with exertion of energy involved in fervent prayer. Seeking our personal comfort does not reflect the intense longing of the heart of God, who is "not willing that any should perish" (2 Pet. 3:9). It does not relate to Jesus' love, who, even now, always "lives to make intercession" for us (Heb. 7:25).

OUR DESPERATE NEED

Many American Christians are placing their trust in our stable government, good economy, and the sense of "godliness by association" with their church programs. Others have been lulled to sleep by their prosperity. We have good doctors and hospitals, so prayer for healing is not our first recourse. We have a good educational system and a great job market so that we don't feel the need to pray for our financial provision. As a result, many Christians in our nation do not follow the instruction of Scripture to "trust in the Lord with all your heart, and lean not on your own understanding; in all your ways acknowledge Him, and He shall direct your paths" (Prov. 3:5-6).

In contrast, my African friends, who learned to pray fervently through sheer necessity, are filled with zeal to establish the Kingdom of God in their nations, overthrowing the destructive kingdom of darkness oppressing these nations. As a result of their selfless commitment to prayer, their nations are being transformed. Some of these nations have Christian presidents and prime ministers, and government officials look to the church to solve social problems.

As American believers, we need to be willing to sacrifice and commit to fervent prayer to birth the purposes of God. We need to focus on the purpose of the Church—prayer—and set our eyes on the harvest. In this way we will establish the Kingdom of God in the earth.

In the American church, every year the number of born-again Christians is decreasing. Instead of allowing this sad reality to intensify their focus on God in prayer, church leaders cast about for some novel approach or strategy that will bring in the harvest. The American church desperately needs to experience revival and the transforming power of God. Our nation needs to be saved from secularism, liberal lifestyles, and the occult and other false religions. God's hand can move against these and other evils in our land only as believers begin to focus their hearts on God's purposes, interceding for souls and bringing down satanic forces that are working in our nation.

FOCUSED ON EVERYTHING BUT PRAYER

Jesus instructed His disciples: "The harvest truly is plentiful, but the laborers are few. Therefore *pray the Lord of the harvest* to send out laborers into His harvest" (Matt. 9:37-38). Too many American churches have done everything but pray. They study intellectual approaches; they strategize; they organize campaigns. But they avoid the truly demanding work of the Kingdom that gets supernatural results—*focused prayer*. It takes energy to pray; it requires sacrifice and commitment. Yet, this simple matter of commitment to prayer seems to threaten our American "independence."

Yonggi Cho prays three times a day every day. He says also that before going into the pulpit he prays three hours. There are people praying at his Prayer Mountain for days and weeks at a time. Every single day there are 25,000 people there praying! And they have been doing this for 25 years. They have learned the power in focusing on God alone and vocally declaring the promises of God, and they experience God's miraculous power manifest in their lives, in the lives of those they love, and in their nation.

Pride or Authority?

One of satan's tactics to keep us from focused prayer is to convince us that such intense prayer with authority is *prideful*. His reasoning goes something like, "Who do you think you are to declare victory over sickness, the devil, and other negative circumstances?" Then he will accuse you of your recent sin or general lack of holiness. Remember, he is the accuser of the brethren. We must understand that it is not prideful to pray with authority; it is obedience to God's Word.

Jesus came to "destroy the works of the devil" (1 John 3:8). And, as believers, He gave us authority to cast out demons, heal the sick, and establish the Kingdom of God in the earth (see Mark 16:17-18). Prayer that is anything less than that is a religious façade, which the devil promotes. Empty of power and authority, it fails to reap the harvest of souls that God intends for us to reap.

---

*We must understand that
it is not prideful to pray with authority.*

As God begins to move in congregations who have prepared their hearts to become new wineskins, some people will not immediately enter into vocal, fervent prayer. They will sit back and watch for a while, not willing for the change required to enter in. But for those who are yearning for a fresh empowerment in prayer, there will be a willingness to embrace the "new." They will dare to make the paradigm shift necessary to abandon their old wineskin of traditional prayer. They will use the authority God gives for calling on Him, with wonderful results. The Scriptures exhort us to submit our lives to God and resist the devil, and he will flee from us (see James 4:7). Little by little, even the most timid believer can enter into this new dimension of corporate prayer, rejoicing in the freedom to lift their focused prayer to God alone.

ENDNOTE

1. "At Ease in Zion" from *Keil & Delitzsch Commentary on the Old Testament*, New Updated Edition, Electronic Database. Copyright © 1996 by Hendrickson Publishers, Inc.

CHAPTER 14

CHANGING YOUR ATMOSPHERE

Creating a Spiritual Climate

A ccording to Jessie Penn-Lewis, who chronicled the phenomenal Welsh revival at the turn of the 20th century, the Spirit of God moved upon the unsaved in converting power as soon as the Christians in a particular church or specific meeting were in unity. He did not wait for all the churches to fall into line, but moved mightily when even a single congregation was brought into one accord with His will.[1] When the proper *atmosphere* was created through prayer, God moved in power. They understood the power of what they called a "charged atmosphere." Penn-Lewis concluded, "We don't need more prayer meetings. We need for people to learn how to pray."[2]

DEVELOPING A SPIRITUAL ATMOSPHERE

No one element of culture, lifestyle, or value systems forms a spiritual atmosphere of a family, a church, a community, or a nation. It is a complex mix of functioning "layers," much like layers of air in the earth's atmosphere. If even one layer becomes toxic or out of balance, the entire atmosphere can be compromised, affecting our happiness, safety, and security.

Complex Factors

There are many interrelated factors that create the spiritual environment in which we live. We have noted that the Bible characterizes the atmosphere of the Kingdom of God as "righteousness and peace and joy in the Holy Spirit" (Rom. 14:17). It is an atmosphere of love, forgiveness, light, and abundant life. The Scriptures characterize the atmosphere of the kingdom of satan as an environment of darkness, robbery, destruction, and death. We have noted that, according to the Scriptures, satan's whole modus operandi is to steal, kill, and destroy (see John 10:10).

When we observe the majority of television and movie productions dealing with murder, death, fear, illicit sex, and unlawful intrigue, we should realize which kingdom is establishing the "atmosphere" of the media. If we choose to watch these portrayals of the kingdom of darkness, we invite that kingdom to influence our lives. Even the newscasts and documentaries make their leading stories the crime and morbidity of the day. Without even considering the cynicism with which they address religious issues, we understand that the atmosphere of the media is not overtly influenced by the Kingdom of God.

Other factors that contribute to a nation's spiritual atmosphere are political, economic, and social. People living without God pursue their own agendas, influencing entire cultures. The Scriptures teach that the devil is the "prince of the power of the air, the spirit who now works in the sons of disobedience" (Eph. 2:2). This evil spiritual power works in the minds and hearts of people who are alienated from God, to create an ungodly and dangerous atmosphere and climate for families, communities, and entire nations.

Our American culture has gone through dramatic changes in the past few decades. For example, when I was a child I remember the freedom I had to walk to school and to play with my friends in almost any neighborhood we chose. We lived in a safe environment of responsible adults. However, it is no longer safe for our children to be unsupervised by an adult anywhere. In many areas, adults are not even safe. Our culture has changed; the atmosphere has become dangerous, resulting in missing children and adults, drug crimes, and other destructive behavior.

CHALLENGING THE DEVIL

Too many Christians have not used their authority in prayer to challenge the devil's inroads into our schools, our youth culture, our political agendas, or social standards. We have allowed a continual downward spiral of our culture away from the healthy atmosphere of "one nation under God." We have become a nation that promotes all manner of ungodly lifestyles. The change in our nation's atmosphere has resulted in a toxic climate, where even the public celebration of Christmas is now at risk.

We discussed the fact that the third dimension of this world is controlled by the fourth dimension—the spiritual realm. And we understand that, as Christians, we have the power of the Holy Spirit dwelling within us. He wants to manifest the

Kingdom of God in every area of our lives. As we learn to yield to Him, He can use us to change the atmosphere in which we live through prayer and obedience to the Kingdom principles. For example, we have the privilege of voting into office righteous leaders, who will govern according to God's principles.

The change in our nation's atmosphere
has resulted in a toxic climate.

God's Kingdom of love, peace, joy, and righteousness desires to reign in our mortal lives, bringing light, life, and prosperity to all He touches. Meanwhile the kingdom of darkness strives to bring its destruction into our lives to undermine the God of love. How we respond to these spiritual influences of the fourth dimension will determine the kind of atmosphere we live in. Evil spirits work to sow anger, bitterness, hatred, and discord in our homes, our churches, and in our places of employment. The Holy Spirit works in and through us to influence the atmosphere for good, to fulfill God's loving will.

CREATING A CLIMATE

When an atmosphere is established over a period of time, it becomes a *climate*. A climate is a predictable and prevailing set of conditions that govern a region. I live in a temperate climate where we enjoy four distinctly different seasons: spring, summer, fall, and winter. The signs of spring are welcomed after the cold of winter, and fall promises a respite from the summer heat. Yet, all the seasons are predictable, occurring approximately at the same time each year. They are part of the established climate for our region, which allows for certain agricultural industry and other climate-related activities to prosper.

In a spiritual climate,
predictable and prevailing conditions govern.

Similarly, in a spiritual climate, predictable and prevailing conditions govern. Your mind is a "region" where a spiritual climate prevails. If you cultivate negative thinking patterns of anger or fear, you will establish a predictable and prevailing set of conditions that govern your thinking.

If the climate of your family spews out vitriolic gases of hate language and disrespect, you will live in a toxic atmosphere of unhappiness. If there is no change to that atmosphere, it will become a predictable, destructive climate. The result will be a break-up of relationships. Hurting people find themselves searching for a more inhabitable atmosphere. The same thing is true in a church, a community, and even a nation. Developing a positive spiritual climate is imperative for the well-being of all people.

IMPACTING CULTURE

This understanding of creating a spiritual climate gives prayer its true significance. For it is through prayer alone that a godly atmosphere or spiritual influence can be brought to bear on the ungodly climate that threatens our peace and tranquility. Whether that climate is in our own minds, in our homes, our churches, or communities, we need to create the elements of a godly atmosphere through prayer in order to live in peace. It is the spiritual realm that impacts life, for good or bad, on every level. On a national level, the process for establishing a culture can be stated simply: *An atmosphere sustained becomes a climate; a climate sustained becomes a culture.*

For example, in Las Vegas the atmosphere for gambling has long been established. Everyone associates casinos and gambling with the mention of this city. The climate of the city is governed by night life, characterized by its partying atmosphere. It is accurate to say that the culture of Las Vegas is governed by its identity as a gambling atmosphere.

In Iraq, the dictator Saddam Hussein created a culture of fear and death, distrust, and suppression of the human spirit. The entire nation of 25 million people suffered under this oppression, as they breathed the toxic atmosphere of cruelty and unrestrained violence. The basis of their culture was formed by a lack of freedom to express their views for fear of reprisal during the 30-year reign of this cruel dictator.

When Dr. David Yonggi Cho founded his church in Korea, he began with only a few very poor people meeting together in a battered tent. They hardly had enough food to eat. Then the Lord revealed to Dr. Cho the reality of living in the fourth dimension. He began to pray for the manifestation of God's Kingdom to come to earth, believing God wanted to meet every need of our humanity, according to His Word. Slowly, as he preached the truth of God's Kingdom to the people, the atmosphere began to change. People began to receive miracles of finances and healing from God, and their faith increased to ask God for more. They prayed for souls and God began to save their families, their employers, their friends.

Living in an atmosphere of faith in God's Word created a prosperous climate, where the prevailing power of God was predictable, meeting the needs of His people. They have dedicated their lives to prayer; it is their first priority. They pray all night every Friday night. Their congregation prays every morning at 5:30 A.M. As a result, they have impacted their entire culture, seeing many lives lifted from poverty to enjoy the blessing of God, including financial success.

---

*Living in an atmosphere of faith in God's Word
created a prosperous climate.*

Now, as the largest church in the world, it is reported that there are 10,000 millionaires in the church and several billionaires. People are healed weekly. God has moved them into the dimension of receiving spiritual dreams and visions, which is the language of the Holy Spirit. They are impacting, not only their nation, with the power of the gospel, but many nations of the world.[3] Yonggi Cho began to change the atmosphere of a small group of people 50 years ago with the truth of the gospel. Today, an entirely new climate has been established, which is creating a different culture, one that exhibits the Kingdom of God. Now, millionaires are praying through the purposes of God and bringing thousands into His Kingdom every year.

HOW TO CHANGE YOUR ATMOSPHERE

In order for you to change the atmosphere and create a godly climate, you simply let the devil know that he is not going to dominate the atmosphere. Refuse to allow it. Do not be intimidated. You cannot negotiate with the devil. Declare the biblical grounds for victory over the enemy: "Therefore submit to God. Resist the devil and he will flee from you. Draw near to God and He will draw near to you" (James 4:7-8a). As we commit our lives to the tireless work of prayer, we understand that we have the responsibility to change the atmosphere through declaring and proclaiming God's Word.

Pray With Authority

As we have mentioned, prayer in another dimension is authoritative. Authoritative prayer crowds out the forces of darkness that try to settle in and create an oppressive, evil atmosphere in a life or situation. You learn to take authority over the encroachment of the enemy into your godly atmosphere and climate. As a believer, it is your responsibility to expose and apprehend the works of darkness. Carlos Annacondia calls this prayer work "unmasking satan."

Authoritative prayer crowds out the forces of darkness.

Satan is a deceiver, a robber, a murderer. The Scriptures declare that "for this purpose the Son of God was manifested, that He might destroy the works of the devil" (1 John 3:8b). In fulfilling the Great Commission that Jesus gave to all believers, our calling is to bind, cast out, or disallow every work and purpose of the enemy. Rescuing souls from the supernatural powers of darkness that blind their minds and keep them from the truth requires that we use the authority in prayer that Jesus gives to us. God is not going to do for us what He has told us to do.

Jesus taught His disciples: "I will give you the keys of the kingdom of heaven, and whatever you bind on earth will be bound in heaven, and whatever you loose on earth will be loosed in heaven" (Matt. 16:19). We have to act on that authority and bind the works of satan in the earth. We *ourselves* must deal with demonic influences that try to poison the atmosphere in which we live. He has given us His Word, but we have to speak it forth with authority. Jesus made it very clear that we have authority over the devil:

> *And He said to them, "I saw Satan fall like lightning from heaven. Behold, I give you the authority to trample on serpents and scorpions, and over all the power of the enemy, and nothing shall by any means hurt you"* (Luke 10:18-19).

The Obedience Factor

When Jesus gave His disciples the Great Commission, He first declared: "All power is given unto Me in heaven and in earth" (Matt. 28:18 KJV). We are empowered to pray for the Kingdom of God to come to earth because all power has been given to our Lord. He followed that statement with a command to obedience: "Go ye therefore." In my book, *I Saw Satan Fall Like Lightning*, I call this the "obedience factor":

> Obedience is the basis for walking in authority. Though this may seem to be an obvious fact, it cannot be over-stated...If we expect to walk in divine authority over the power of the enemy, we have to first of all surrender in obedience to the authority of God over our lives. It is in that place of obedience that faith is born...The Lord has a plan for His church to understand how authority is

released through obedience...Our obedience to His will is the key to releasing His divine anointing throughout our lives.[4]

Obedience is the basis for walking in authority.

Dr Cho writes: "Through dominion in the fourth dimension, the realm of faith, you can give order to your circumstances and situations, give beauty to the ugly and chaotic, and healing to the hurt and suffering."[5] The necessity of declaring the Word of God to change the atmosphere is a vital key to prayer that "avails much." (Please refer to Chapter 16 for specific examples of praying the truth of God's Word.) Do not allow the enemy to infringe his deadly atmosphere on you by keeping you silent, apathetic, and complacent. Learn to fight the good fight of faith with the tools God has given you to create your spiritual atmosphere and prevailing climate.

MIRACLES ARE MY DAY JOB

Dr. Charles Agyin Asare is Senior Pastor of Headquarters Church of the World Miracle Church International, one of the largest and fastest growing local churches in Ghana. He testifies that eight people have been raised from the dead through his ministry. His local congregation, numbering 23,000 recently, is growing dramatically, and he ministers to crowds of more than 100,000 in many places, recording healings and miracles.

As Dr. Asare has learned to minister in the realm of miracles, he understands that day-time miracles require night-time praying. He refers to Jesus' pattern of ministry, praying whole nights alone, and then ministering to multitudes during the day:

> *However, the report went around concerning Him all the more; and great multitudes came together to hear, and to be healed by Him of their infirmities. So He Himself often withdrew into the wilderness and prayed* (Luke 5:15-16).

Dr. Agyin Asare writes in his book, *Power in Prayer*, that it is demonic forces that are keeping people from being saved as well as from being established in Christ as new believers. Therefore he spends most of his time praying down the strongholds that blind and bind people from the truth of the gospel, rather than trying to talk to people to convince them of their need for salvation.[6] The Scriptures support this understanding that people are blinded from the truth by the devil. The apostle Paul declared, "But even if our gospel is veiled, it is veiled to those who are perishing, whose minds the god of this age has blinded" (2 Cor. 4:3-4a).

"Demonic forces are keeping people from being saved."
—*Bishop Agyin Asare*

Of course, preaching is part of the way God has chosen to bring the truth to the lost. Yet, it is as we release the atmosphere of faith and light through prayer, bringing down demonic strongholds of the "god of this world," that people are free to hear the truth. Then they can choose between the darkness they are living in and the warmth of love they experience in a godly atmosphere. Through fervent prayer, the lost can respond to the truth of the Word they hear through preaching of the gospel. Agyin Asare describes how he prepares for his great crusades:

> Before our crusades I spend two to three days in fasting and prayer...I sometimes do it alone; at times I pray and fast with my team. In each of these days, we deal with the principalities that rule the communities. We spend at least eight hours every day in praying, asking that God will save souls, that the demonized will be set free and the sick healed. During our crusades, I spend 3-5 hours every day in prayer asking God to meet the needs of the people. Every afternoon...I lock myself in the room from 2:00 P.M. I rest and pray till the crusade and when I get onto the platform the miracles just take place. I do not fast during my crusades for I need the physical strength to preach, pray and cast out devils. I do the fasts before.[7]

> Pastor Wisdom Dafeamakpor concludes: "When Bishop Asare comes onto the platform he simply speaks and the sick get healed."[8] Bishop Asare's response is, "One thing I know is that if you do your homework in private prayer, you do not need to pray long publicly. Nobody is more powerful than their prayer life."[9]

Sogakope, Ghana, a town of 7000, is noted for its black magic. Bishop Asare said he prayed three hours in the morning with his team and three hours personally in the afternoon during this crusade. Each night a crowd of 40,000 came to the crusade. The ruling witches spread a dark powder around the town, so that anyone who stepped on the powder would become blind, deaf and dumb, or crippled. But as the healing miracles increased in the crusade, even the chief of the town attended, saying, "I have heard of the power of God at work in my town and of crowds bigger than we have ever seen here. So I came to see for myself."[10]

PRACTICAL STEPS TO CREATING A GODLY ATMOSPHERE

I have not found a more concise and instructive guide for the practical steps involved in changing your spiritual atmosphere than that given by Tudor Bismarck of Harare, Zimbabwe. In his message, "Atmospheres and Climates," from which we have drawn the principles discussed here, he presents a three-step approach:[11]

1. **Cast out the devil.** Disallow his work, his opposition, his accusations. Apply the blood of Jesus and speak in the power of His name, breaking curses and refusing the bondage he endeavors to bring into your life.

2. **Bind the doctrines of devils.** People develop thinking patterns that have been imposed by the devil through spirits of witchcraft or seducing spirits, such as the Jezebel spirit. The apostle Paul told Timothy what to expect in the last days: "Now the Spirit speaketh expressly, that in the latter times some shall depart from the faith, giving heed to seducing spirits, and doctrines of devils; speaking lies in hypocrisy; having their conscience seared with a hot iron" (1 Tim. 4:1-2 KJV). These doctrines of devils have to be displaced by the truth of God's

Word, ministered under the anointing of the Holy Spirit.

3. **Deal with territorial or regional spirits.** Spiritual strongholds that rule communities, cities, and entire cultures must be brought down through strategic prayer and fasting. Let the devil know he is not going to dominate the atmosphere of your community. Refuse to tolerate his mind-set, attitudes, and ungodliness. Refuse to allow it.

Through aggressive prayer we can change the atmosphere of oppression that the enemy tries to establish in our homes, our churches, our communities, and even our nation. We can re-establish an atmosphere and develop a climate where the work of God can be accomplished and where people who are bound by satan can be set free. God desires that we live in the "clean air" atmosphere of His Kingdom, composed of right-eousness, peace, and joy in the Holy Ghost.

ENDNOTES

1. Jessie Penn-Lewis, *The Awakening in Wales* (Dorset, England: The Overcomer Literature Trust, n.d.), p. 68.

2. Ibid.

3. Tudor Bismark Ministries, Jabula-New Life Ministries, 445 East FM1382, Suite 3-371, Cedar Hill, Texas 75104, www.Tudor Bismark.org.

4. Sue Curran, *I Saw Satan Fall Like Lightning* (Lake Mary, FL: Creation House, 1998), pp. 14-15.

5. Dr. David Yonggi Cho, *The Fourth Dimension* (Gainesville, FL: Bridge-Logos, 1979).

6. Charles Agyin Asare, *Power in Prayer, Taking Your Blessings by Force* (Typeset by Prince Stanilas Asare, Produced by His Printing Hoornaar, The Netherlands, 2001, ISBN 9988-7530-5-5).

7. Ibid., p. 91.

8. Ibid., p. 97.

9. Ibid.

10. Ibid.

11. Tudor Bismark Ministries, Jabula-New Life Ministries, 445 East FM1382, Suite 3-371, Cedar Hill, Texas 75104, www.Tudor Bismark.org.

CHAPTER 15

PRAY THE LORD OF THE HARVEST

Making Prophetic Declarations

I received a World News item from Sweden recently that gave the following incredible statistics regarding the harvest of souls in Ukraine: "When Ukraine gained independence from the former Soviet Union in 1991, there were 250,000 evangelical Christians in the country. Today there are 3 million. That is 1,000 percent growth in a decade."[1] Earlier, I mentioned Pastor Sunday Adelaja, a Nigerian who has established a church of 30,000 members in Ukraine. He describes his people as "God-seekers." They live a lifestyle of prayer, making it the priority of their Christian service. As they "pray the Lord of the harvest" (Matt. 9:38), breaking the power of darkness that blinds people to the truth of the gospel, God is sending in a phenomenal harvest of souls.

Pastor Adelaja has suffered persecution at the hands of the Ukrainian government. The KGB pursued him and forbade him to travel out of the country for several years. They tried to deport him, and to otherwise hinder his ministry. These government officials do not believe there is any hope for a drug addict to be rehabilitated. Pastor Adelaja has many former drug addicts in his church, having been set free from their destructive lifestyle, who are now serving Christ. So, Adelaja invited the government officials to come to his church to see 1,000 former drug addicts who are free to serve God. Through the power of prayer, souls have been rescued from destructive lifestyles, which no drug rehabilitation program could accomplish.

He describes his people as "God-seekers."

Archbishop Duncan-Williams concurs: "If we will pray, God will send in the harvest." He tells of a great campaign they hosted in Ghana where 3,000 people came forward to receive Christ as their Savior. Yet, only 100 of these people became established in his church. He asked the Lord what he had done wrong. The Lord spoke to him, "Your organization and your preaching were fine, but you did not undergird the campaign with prayer." Since Duncan-Williams learned that the secret to winning souls is prayer, he has established several megachurches in Ghana and is reaping a harvest in other nations of the world. The battle for souls is spiritual and cannot be won by preaching alone. Fervent, travailing prayer is absolutely necessary for reaping the harvest.

PRAYING FOR REVIVAL

Church history records that great revival movements were preceded by intense prayer of saints who were hungry to have the presence of God. We mentioned that in the great Welsh revival of 1904, led by Evan Roberts and others, fervent, intense prayer preceded the wonderful ingathering of souls, which impacted their entire nation.

Fervent, travailing prayer is absolutely necessary for reaping the harvest.

Frank Bartleman describes an intense prayer effort that preceded the Pentecostal movement as well, which was birthed at the Azusa Street Mission in Los Angeles, California, in 1906. It was not through great preaching or evangelistic programs that God poured out His Spirit during that great revival; it was in answer to intense, fervent prayer. Having heard of the outpouring of God's Spirit in Wales, these Christians sought God with all their hearts to experience that kind of revival. As a result, the worldwide influence of Pentecostals was birthed. They established many thousands of churches, great missions works and Bible schools, and reaped a wonderful harvest of souls in many nations.[7]

Only prayer can break the chains of blindness, ignorance, and oppression with which satan binds people's hearts and minds. The devil knows that if he can keep us from praying, this strongman can keep his possessions secure—the souls of lost men and women. The anointing of the Holy Spirit is released upon men and women who seek God with all their hearts in prayer.

Pastor Benny Hinn understands that the anointing of the Holy Spirit for miracles of salvation and healing is released, not only through studying the Word, but through prayer. While we cannot negate the power of the Word of God, it must be bathed in prayer to release its power into lives for salvation. Pastor Hinn shuts himself in his room for several hours before each service of his large crusades, waiting on God in prayer to release the anointing of the Holy Spirit. It is that anointing that allows people to respond to the preached Word and to receive miracles of healing.

PRAYING IN PRISON

You are familiar with the biblical account of Paul and Silas, who were beaten and thrown into the inner prison because of their witness for Christ. They began to pray and sing praises to God at midnight. Their declarations of the power and love of God in that dark place loosed them and brought salvation to many:

> *And when they had laid many stripes on them, they threw them into prison, commanding the jailer to keep them securely. Having received such a charge, he put them into the inner prison and fastened their feet in the stocks. But at midnight Paul and Silas were praying and singing hymns to God, and the prisoners were listening to them. Suddenly there was a great earthquake, so that the foundations of the prison were shaken; and immediately all the doors were opened and everyone's chains were loosed* (Acts 16:23-26).

Such miraculous intervention through prayer was a norm for the lives of these first Christians. They lived lives abandoned to prayer for the salvation of souls and the establishing of the Kingdom of God in the earth. When the jailer realized what had happened, he committed his life, and his entire household, to the Christ who had delivered Paul and Silas.

Through prayer, not only were these apostles set free from their prison chains, but souls were won to the Kingdom. Permanent victories must be won in the Spirit through the supernatural means of prayer. The Scriptures declare: "For whatever is born of God overcomes the world. And this is the victory that has overcome the world—our faith" (1 John 5:4). Only what is born of God through faith will overcome the world. Intellectual assent to a religious creed is not the same as being infused with the supernatural life of God when we are born again. It is travailing prayer that brings souls to birth in the Kingdom of God.

PRAYING FOR LABORERS

Jesus taught His disciples how to pray for the harvest. He told them to pray to the Lord of the Harvest and, specifically, for the laborers in the harvest:

> But when He saw the multitudes, He was moved with compassion for them, because they were weary and scattered, like sheep having no shepherd. Then He said to His disciples, "The harvest truly is plentiful, but the laborers are few. Therefore pray the Lord of the harvest to send out laborers into His harvest" (Matthew 9:36-38).

It is important to note that it is God's harvest. The problem is not with the harvest, but with the laborers. It was John who recorded Jesus' command to "lift up your eyes and look at the fields, for they are already white for harvest!" (John 4:35). I believe the Lord wants us to look at the harvest until we see what He sees, allowing His compassion for lost and hurting people to fill our hearts. Then He expects us to pray to the Lord of the harvest so that laborers will be released under the direction of the One who knows how to reap the harvest. The Lord of the harvest will anoint laborers—each of us—to move into the fields in His timing and wisdom so that the crops will not be damaged or lost.

It is important to note that it is God's harvest.

I am certain that we do not disagree with the instructions of Jesus to pray concerning the harvest. It is just that we don't get around to it. When we have a desire to be involved in reaping the harvest, we do everything but pray. We study, we train, we strategize, we clamor after any fresh evangelistic approach that seems to be working. While these efforts are not wrong, they will never be a substitute for prayer.

Preaching is not enough to reap the harvest. Prayer releases the anointing of the Holy Spirit to open blind eyes and allow them to see the truth. The Scriptures declare of the first disciples: "And they went out and preached everywhere, the Lord working with them and confirming the word through the accompanying signs" (Mark 16:20). The Spirit of God works through the Word of God as we release His power in our lives through prayer. In his book, *Prayer: Key to Revival*, Yonggi Cho wrote: "Americans pray for revival and when revival comes they stop praying, so they always lose the revival."[3]

We are not greater than our Master. Jesus was the Word Incarnate on this earth, but He did not do any miracles until the Holy Spirit filled Him with power at His baptism. Jesus was filled with the Holy Spirit before He began His public ministry. After His baptism, He prayed often, spending entire nights alone in prayer. He is our example of how to do the works of God in the earth:

However, the report went around concerning Him all the more; and great multitudes came together to hear, and to be healed by Him of their infirmities. So He Himself often withdrew into the wilderness and prayed (Luke 5:15-16).

A lifestyle of prayer enables us to see life from God's perspective, to know His heart of love for the lost. The Scriptures declare that He is "not willing that any should perish but that all should come to repentance" (2 Pet. 3:9). As we touch His heart, we will experience a passionate desire to bring men and women to Christ. According to Duncan-Williams, "If we are not praying, we do not have the ability to look into the mind of God and 'download' His power into the earth."

Prayer is not a feeling, an inspiration, or an option. To be effective in the harvest, as well as every other area of life, prayer must become a way of life. It requires discipline, an establishing of a structure of prayer into our lifestyles, and becoming people of consistent prayer. The Scriptures give a powerful insight into the cumulative power of the prayers of the saints in Heaven. In the Book of Revelation we read:

Then another angel, having a golden censer, came and stood at the altar. He was given much incense, that he should offer it with the prayers of all the saints upon the golden altar which was before the throne. And the smoke of the incense, with the prayers of the saints, ascended before God from the angel's hand. Then the angel took the censer, filled it with fire from the altar, and threw it to the earth. And there were noises, thunderings, lightnings, and an earthquake (Revelation 8:3-5).

In a heavenly way, our prayers are collected in Heaven and kept in vessels until they can be poured back on the earth, where they are accompanied by the fire of God. Whatever else we understand from this passage, it shows clearly that our prayers are an investment in the heavenly realm, to be used by God for His purposes. As Duncan-Williams states it, "Too many people have not invested their lives in prayer; their prayer lives are in a state of bank 'overdraft.'" Our prayers have eternal value, which cannot be accrued unless we commit our lives to consistent prayer, individually and corporately.

Our prayers are an investment in the heavenly realm.

How to Pray for Souls[4]

While it is clear to many that they should pray for souls, often they don't know how to pray beyond, "Lord, please save my son." It is all right to ask God for salvation for souls, but as we have learned, there are powerful keys to effective prayer that we can use in praying for souls as well. For example, we can ask the Holy Spirit to do His wonderful convicting work in their lives, as the Scriptures explain:

And when He has come, He will convict the world of sin, and of righteousness, and of judgment: of sin, because they do not believe in Me; of righteousness, because I go to My Father and you see Me no more; of judgment, because the ruler of this world is judged (John 16:8-11).

Have you ever tried to convince someone of being a sinner and needing to receive Christ as their Savior? If so, you know that without the working of the Holy Spirit to convict that person, you will only offend and alienate them further from the truth. It is the work of the Holy Spirit to draw hearts and to convict them of sin. When He shines His light of truth on hearts, people begin to see themselves like never before. They come to repentance, recognizing their need of a Savior. Praying the promise of God to send the Holy Spirit to convict of sin is a powerful way to pray for souls.

Pray the "Portion" of God

In praying for lost souls we can also ask for the goodness of God to be their portion, as the Old Testament writer declared:

Through the Lord's mercies we are not consumed, because His compassions fail not. They are new every morning; great is Your faithfulness. "The Lord is my portion," says my soul, "Therefore I hope in Him!" The Lord is good to those who wait for Him, to the soul who seeks Him (Lamentations 3:22-25).

Praying that the Lord will be the portion for lost souls is asking for the goodness of God—His mercies—to come to them. The apostle Paul declared that it is the "goodness of God" that leads souls to repentance (Rom. 2:4). It is God's mercy and long-suffering that seeks to enlighten darkened minds and hardened hearts, which are alienated from the love of God.

We should not just assume the goodness of God, but can ask in prayer for His mercies upon those who need to be saved. Pray for the goodness of God to reach out to the lost person for whom you are praying. Ask Him to reveal His mercies to them, causing them to come to repentance.

Pray the Promises of God

Promises are just that—promises. They do not have intrinsic power but are statements of the will and purpose of God *waiting to be activated by believing prayer*. What are the promises of God concerning salvation of the lost? We know that He is not willing that any should perish. And the Scriptures clearly state that whoever believes in Him will not perish:

> For God so loved the world that He gave His only begotten Son, that whoever believes in Him should not perish but have everlasting life. For God did not send His Son into the world to condemn the world, but that the world through Him might be saved (John 3:16-17).

The apostle Paul wrote: "Whoever calls on the name of the Lord shall be saved" (Rom. 10:13). We can ask God to work by His Spirit to convict souls and help them to call on the name of the Lord. Remember, it is a spiritual birth they need, which is only available as the realm of the Spirit—the fourth dimension—is brought to bear on their lives. We can facilitate that supernatural encounter through fervent, travailing prayer for souls.

PRAY THE POWER OF GOD

Living in a cultural climate that promotes self-help on every level, it is not surprising that people try to "save themselves" in one way or another. Through doing good deeds, performing religious acts, or following philanthropic pursuits, many feel they are sure to please God with their actions. They need to realize what the apostle Paul taught about salvation:

For I am not ashamed of the gospel of Christ, for it is the power of God to salvation for everyone who believes, for the Jew first and also for the Greek (Romans 1:16).

Believing the gospel of Christ by faith, repenting of our sin and accepting forgiveness through His blood, is the power of salvation. Any other "source" of self-help is simply a false security, which is unable to save our souls. The apostle Peter declared that we "are kept by the power of God through faith for salvation ready to be revealed in the last time." (1 Pet. 1:5). It is the power of God that saves us and it is His power that keeps us as well.

Living in a false security of their own "goodness" is a trap of the devil to keep lost souls from knowing they are lost—alienated from the love of God. We must pray that they will hear the gospel and be able to respond to its claims. Only by believing in Christ as Savior can souls be birthed into the Kingdom of God. That is the power of God for salvation, and we can pray for God to move in power in their lives.

Pray the Purposes of God

We have discussed the power in praying the Word of God, which reveals the purposes of God for mankind. When praying for lost souls, we can proclaim the purposes of God for salvation. For example, when the Lord appeared to Saul on the road to Damascus, He declared to him the purpose for his life and ministry, which would fulfill the purposes of God:

> I am Jesus, whom you are persecuting...I have appeared to you for this purpose, to make you a minister and a witness both of the things which you have seen and of the things which I will yet reveal to you. I will deliver you from the Jewish people, as well as from the Gentiles, to whom I now send you, to open their eyes, in order to turn them from darkness to light, and from the power of Satan to God, that they may receive forgiveness of sins and an inheritance among those who are sanctified by faith in Me (Acts 26:15-18).

It is God's purpose to open the eyes of those living in spiritual darkness and set them free from the power of satan, to give them forgiveness of sins and an inheritance through faith. When we pray the will of God, we know that God hears us and answers those prayers (see 1 John 3:21-22). Praying the purposes of God for our families, our churches, our communities, and our nation is a powerful way to reap the harvest God wants to give to us.

Pray the "Person" of God

We can remind God in prayer of His love, His mercies, and His longsuffering. We can call on our Redeemer and appeal to

His goodness. For example, we can ask that as He spared Ninevah of old, He intervene in a similar manner for our "lost" situations. When Abraham interceded for his nephew Lot, he appealed to the righteousness of God, pleading with Him: "Would You also destroy the righteous with the wicked?" (Gen. 18:23). Because of Abraham's intercession, God made a way to spare Lot, though He brought judgment on the wicked city of Sodom where Lot and his family lived.

Moses appealed to God's name in order to intercede for the wicked nation of Israel. God wanted to wipe them out and raise up another nation from Moses. But Moses pleaded with God to remember His covenant with Abraham, Isaac, and Israel, "Your servants, to whom You swore by Your own self, and said to them, 'I will multiply your descendants as the stars of heaven'" (Exod. 32:13). In one of the most amazing verses of Scripture in the Bible, we read: "So the Lord relented from the harm which He said He would do to His people" (Exod. 32:14). Moses' intercession, based on who God is, spared an entire nation the wrath of God they deserved to receive.

As we give ourselves to the reading of the Word and prayer, we discover God's heart. The more deeply intertwined our hearts become with the heart of God, the more we understand how to pray the will of God for every situation, and especially for lost souls.

PRAYING BIBLICAL PRAYERS

Unless you are convinced that prayer is the means by which you have a definite and necessary part in fulfilling the promises of God, your commitment to prayer will falter. When you embrace that reality, you will need to be equipped to pray biblical prayers in the will of God. To help you enter into a new dimension of effective prayer, I have included in the last chapter a list of declarations of faith—Prayer Points— for your use in prayer. (See Chapter 16.) These Prayer Points were originally published by my African mentors, and I want to refer you to their more comprehensive works as well (see Bibliography). They are giving the Body of Christ wonderful tools, based on declarations from the Scriptures, to help equip you in learning to pray more powerfully—in another dimension.

It is of little use to read this book and understand the keys to prayer in another dimension if you do not receive practical tools with which to experience that dimension of prayer. As you choose to make prayer a priority in your life, it is my prayer that the prophetic declarations compiled here will help launch you into new levels of faith-filled prayer.

I challenge you to begin to make declaration and proclamation concerning your own freedom in prayer and the purposes of God over your life and your family. As you begin to see answers to those prayers, you will be encouraged to pursue the larger purposes of God for your church, community, and nation. You will see your own life transformed to walk in the destiny for which you were born, and you will be able to reap the harvest that God has ordained as your spiritual inheritance.

ENDNOTES

1. World News, February 3, 2005: Geri McGhee, quoting from Charisma (Lake Mary, FL: Strang Communications), February 2005 issue.

2. Jessie Penn-Lewis, *The Awakening in Wales* (Dorset, England: The Overcomer Literature Trust, n.d.).

3. Dr. David Yonggi Cho, *Prayer: Key to Revival* (Waco, TX: Word Books, 1984).

4. Lee Thomas, "Praying Effectively for the Lost," article retrieved from the Internet at www.pelministries.org, accessed on December 7, 2005.

CHAPTER 16

PRAYER POINTS

A Practical Guide

I responded to an invitation to a *Prayer Summit,* hosted by Archbishop Nicholas Duncan-Williams. During that conference, I experienced the power of praying in a focused way, using "prayer points" as a platform for praying God's Word. We prayed all day on Saturday under the direction of prayer leaders. I realized the effectiveness of praying specific, biblical declarations during those powerful prayer services.

I asked the Archbishop for permission to share these prayer points as a spiritual tool for prayer for those to whom I minister. He graciously consented, and I have supplied the following practical guide of biblical declarations that may be utilized as you apply yourself to praying in another dimension.

Rather than praying your thoughts, ideas, or opinions, you can pray the Word of God so that you know you are praying in the will of God. Understanding how important it is to proclaim and declare the Word of God, you can use these tools to help you pray with authority. The devil fears the Word of God, especially when prayed with authority.

These prayer points are adapted from a 21-day concerted effort of prayer and fasting. They will give you a picture of a dedicated and focused people gathering for a season of prayer to seek God for breakthroughs in areas of life that all of us find challenging.

For the sake of exposing you to the atmosphere and practical approach of praying corporately in a Prayer Summit, I have presented them basically as they were used there, with few adaptations. These categories of focused prayer were established through seeking God for His purposes. Then, believers searched the Scriptures to provide the basis of a prayer for each need. In this way, their prayers have a biblical basis, which empowers the proclamations to be made in the will of God.

For more comprehensive Prayer Points materials, I encourage you to obtain other books by Pastor Matthew Ashimolowo and Archbishop Nicholas Duncan-Williams—some of which are listed in the Bibliography. At their web sites you will find other reading materials, which have been very helpful in showing us practical ways to enter into prayer in another dimension.

PRAYER POINTS

Quick Reference

CONFESSION AND REPENTANCE

1.   Pray that the Holy Spirit will bring to your memory every sin you may have committed knowing or unknowingly.

Keep back Your servant also from presumptuous sins; Let them not have dominion over me. Then I shall be blameless, and I shall be innocent of great transgression.

—Psalm 19:13

2.   Confess every sin before God in sincerity and ask for His forgiveness and cleansing by the blood.

If we confess our sins, he is faithful and just to forgive us our sins, and to cleanse us from all unrighteousness.

—1 John 1:9

3.   Stand in the gap and ask forgiveness for the sins of our families and loved ones.

So I sought for a man among them who would make a wall, and stand in the gap before Me on behalf of the land, that I should not destroy it: but I found no one.

—Ezekiel 22:30

4.   Pray that the Lord will enable us to be reconciled with those whom we have offended and with those who have offended us.

A brother offended is harder to win than a strong city, and contentions are like the bars of a castle.

—Proverbs 18:19

5.   Confess your forgiveness and release before God so that your prayers will not be hindered.

And whenever you stand praying, if you have anything against anyone, forgive him, that your Father in Heaven

may also forgive you your trespasses. But if you do not for-
give, neither will your Father in heaven forgive your tres-
passes.

—Mark 11:25–26

Beloved, if our heart does not condemn us, we have confi-
dence toward God. And whatever we ask we receive from
Him...

—1 John 3:21–22

6. Bless your enemies, and pray that God will convict the hearts
   of those harboring offenses against you to forgive.

   But I say to you, love your enemies, bless those who curse
   you, do good to those who hate you, and pray for those who
   spitefully use you and persecute you, that you may be sons
   of your Father in heaven...

   —Matthew 6: 44–45

7. Break the power of the spirit of unforgiveness over your life
   that harbors offense and hinders the power of love.

   But know this, that in the last days perilous times will
   come; For men will be lovers of themselves...unloving,
   unforgiving...lovers of pleasure rather than lovers of God.

   —2 Timothy 3:1–4

8. Employ the voice of the blood of Jesus that speaks better
   things to silence and over-throw every accusation of the
   devil against you.

   But you have come to Mount Zion and to the city of the liv-
   ing God...to Jesus the Mediator of the new covenant, and to
   the blood of sprinkling, that speaks better things than that
   of Abel.

   —Hebrews 12:22–24

...for the accuser of the brethren, who accused them before our God day and night, has been cast down. And they overcame him by the blood of the Lamb and by the word of their testimony, and they did not love their lives to the death.

—Revelation 12:10–11

9.   Ask the Lord to heal you of emotional hurts and pains as a result of bitterness and grief.

The Spirit of the Lord is upon me, because he has anointed me to preach the gospel to the poor; He has sent me to heal the brokenhearted, to proclaim liberty to the captives, and recovery of sight to the blind, to set at liberty those who are oppressed; to proclaim the acceptable year of the Lord.

—Luke 4:18–19

10.   Thank God for His compassion and forgiveness of all the sin in your life.

I, even I, am he that blots out your transgressions for My own sake, and I will not remember your sins.

—Isaiah 43:25

STRATEGIC PRAYER FORCE FOR THE SET GIFT OF THE HOUSE

11.   Pray against every abortive spirit assigned against the pastor and against his/her dream, vision, aspiration and mandate.

12.   Command the womb of the pastor's imagination to be fruitful and to bring forth ideas that will elevate the church and his/her personal life.

13.   Command, through the blood of Jesus, covenant blessings of the womb for the pastor as prophesied for Joseph.

Joseph is a fruitful bough, a fruitful bough by a well; His branches run over the wall...his bow remained in strength, and the arms of his hands were made strong by the hands of the Mighty God of Jacob (From there is the Shepherd, the Stone of Israel), by the God of your father who will help you, and by the Almighty who will bless you with blessings of heaven above, blessings of the deep that lies beneath, blessings of the breasts and of the womb.

—Genesis 49:22–25

14. Reverse the consequences of the iniquities of the father and mother working against the mandate of the pastor to undermine his/her authority.

15. Command a breaking up of every fallow ground and hardness of heart around the pastor and the church.

Sow for yourselves righteousness; Reap in mercy; Break up your fallow ground: for it is time to seek the LORD, till He comes and rains righteousness on you.

—Hosea 10:12

16. Cut off the root of every spirit of jealousy, intimidation, deviation, vexation and envy working against the pastor.

17. Decree, by the blood of the covenant, a corresponding reward and satisfaction from battles both past and present, as in David's victory at Ziklag, and enforce the victory of Calvary on the pastor's present circumstances.

So David recovered all that the Amalekites had carried away...And nothing of theirs was lacking, either small or great, sons or daughters, spoil or anything which they had taken from them; David recovered all.

—1 Samuel 30:18–19

18. Pray against every strange snare or spiritual order assigned by hell to undermine the effectiveness and authority of the pastor.

If it had not been the LORD who was on our side, when men rose up against us...Then the waters would have gone over

*our soul...Our soul has escaped as a bird from the snare of
the fowlers; The snare is broken, and we have escaped. Our
help is in the name of the LORD.*

—Psalm 124:2,4,7–8

19. Quench strange fiery darts shot from hell against the pastor's emotions.

20. Command to halt every diversion of satanic strategy against the pastor.

BREAKING AND UPROOTING CURSES

21. Break the curse of poverty and lack that has been in your family for generations.

*And all these blessings shall come upon you and overtake
you because you obey the voice of the Lord your God...The
LORD will command the blessing on you in your storehous-
es and in all to which you set your hand.*

—Deuteronomy 28:2,8

22. Reverse the curse of dissatisfaction in all things you do.

*The eyes of all look expectantly to You, and You give them
their food in due season. You open Your hand and satisfy
the desire of every living thing.*

—Psalm 145:15–16

23. Break the curse of idol worship in our families.

*Cursed is the one who makes a carved or molded image, an
abomination to the LORD, the work of the hands of the
craftsman, and set it up in secret.. And all the people shall
answer and say, 'Amen!'*

—Deuteronomy 27:15–16

24. Break every militant curse against your business and finances.

Let Your work appear to Your servants, and Your glory to their children. And let the beauty of the LORD our God be upon us, and establish the work of our hands for us; Yes, establish the work of our hands.

—Psalm 90:16–17

25. Break the impact of the curse of incest and the curse of participating in any sexual sin.

Cursed is the one who lies with his father's wife, because he has uncovered his father's bed...Cursed is the one who lies with any kind of animal...Cursed is the one who lies with his sister, the daughter of his father or the daughter of his mother.

—Deuteronomy 27:20–23

26. Break the generational curse that may be hindering you from fulfilling your purpose and calling in life.

In those days they shall say no more: 'The fathers have eaten sour grapes, and the children's teeth are set on edge.' But every one shall die for his own iniquity; every man who eats the sour grapes, his teeth shall be set on edge.

—Jeremiah 31:29–30

You show lovingkindness to thousands, and repay the iniquity of the fathers into the bosom of their children after them—the Great, the Mighty God, whose name is the LORD of hosts. You are great in counsel and mighty in work, for your eyes are open to all the ways of the sons of men, to give everyone according to his ways and according to the fruit of his doings.

—Jeremiah 32:18–19

27. Repent for a lack of commitment and revoke the curse of much labor and less harvest in the name of Jesus.

Now therefore, thus says the LORD of hosts: "Consider your ways! You have sown much, and bring in little...You looked for much, but indeed it came to little...Why?" says the LORD of hosts. "Because of My house that is in ruins, while every one of you runs to his own house."

—Haggai 1:5–6, 9

28. Cancel the curse of sowing without reaping in the name of Jesus

Then the children of Israel did evil in the sight of the LORD. So the LORD delivered them into the hand of Midian...So it was, whenever Israel had sown, Midianites would come up...Then they would encamp against them and destroy the produce of the earth as far as Gaza and leave no sustenance for Israel...

—Judges 6:1, 3–4

29. Cancel the curse that makes people abhor you instead of favoring you.

And I will give this people favor in the sight of the Egyptians; and it shall be, when you go, that you shall not go empty-handed.

—Exodus 3:21

30. Cancel every curse of genetic disease in your family.

Christ has redeemed us from the curse of the law, having become a curse for us(for it is written, "Cursed is everyone who hangs on a tree").

—Galatians 3:13

...who Himself bore our sins in His own body on the tree, that we, having died to sins, might live for righteousness— by whose stripes you were healed.

—1 Peter 2:24

31. Employ the blood of Jesus to negate any curse on your life emanating from conflict with parents.

Cursed is the one who treats his father or his mother with contempt. And all the people shall say, Amen.

—Deuteronomy 27:16

32. Overthrow every curse pronounced against you by false prophets to cause your defeat in battle.

Therefore please come at once, curse this people for me, for they are too mighty for me. Perhaps I shall be able to defeat them and drive them out of the land, for I know that he whom you bless is blessed, and he whom you curse is cursed.

—Numbers 22:6

33. Decree that your enemies will lack the ability to pronounce curses against you.

How shall I curse, whom God hath not cursed? or how shall I defy, whom the LORD hath not defied?

—Numbers 23:8

PRAYING FOR OUR PASTORS

34. Pray that all the pastors will walk in the fullness of the fruits of the spirit, and according to God's perfect plan

But the fruit of the Spirit is love, joy, peace, longsuffering, gentleness, goodness, faith, meekness, temperance: against such there is no law.

—Galatians 5:22–23

35.   Pray that they will overcome all weariness and be renewed by the power of the Holy Spirit.

But those who wait on the LORD shall renew their strength; They shall mount up with wings like eagles, they shall run and not be weary, they shall walk and not faint.

—Isaiah 40:31

36.   Ask God to empower them to walk in holiness, purity, humility and integrity.

Let no man despise thy youth; but be thou an example of the believers, in word, in conversation, in charity, in spirit, in faith, in purity.

—1 Timothy 4:12

37.   Pray that God will broaden their vision and empower them to carry it out with zeal and wisdom. Ask for zeal of the apostle Paul, who declared:

...Not that I have already attained, or am already perfected; but I press on, that I may lay hold of that for which Christ Jesus has also laid hold of me. Brethren, I do not count myself to have apprehended; but one thing I do, forgetting those things which are behind and reaching forward to those things which are ahead, I press toward the goal for the prize of the upward call of God in Christ Jesus.

—Philippians 3:12–14

38.   Employ the covering of the blood of Jesus over the pastors and their families and release divine protection over them.

The LORD shall preserve you from all evil; He shall preserve your soul. The LORD shall preserve your going out and your coming in from this time forth, and even forevermore.

—Psalm 121:7–8

39. Arrest, bind, paralyze and cart out every agent of satan in the church warring against pastors.

No weapon formed against you shall prosper, and every tongue which rises against you in judgment you shall condemn. This is the heritage of the servants of the LORD, and their righteousness is from Me, says the LORD.

—Isaiah 54:17

40. Bind and cast out every spirit of Jezebel warring against the pastors.

...For so it was, while Jezebel massacred the prophets of the LORD, that Obadiah had taken one hundred prophets and hidden them, fifty to a cave, and had fed them with bread and water.

—1 Kings 18:4

41. Pray for unity and love to prevail between pastors and their supporting leaders and the congregations as a whole.

Behold, how good and how pleasant it is for brethren to dwell together in unity!

—Psalm 133:1

42. Pray and overthrow every attack of evil powers on their marriages. Also, pray that love and unity will govern their marriages.

Let your fountain be blessed and rejoice with the wife of your youth.

—Proverbs 5:18

43. Pray that God will raise men and women to support the pastors in all areas of their ministry.

...and Joanna the wife of Chuza, Herod's steward, and Susanna, and many others who provided for Him from their substance.

—Luke 8:3

I am glad about the coming of Stephanas, Fortunatus, and Achaicus, for what was lacking on your part they supplied. For they refreshed my spirit and yours. Therefore acknowledge such men.

—1 Corinthians 16:17–18

INTERCEDING FOR THE CHURCH

44.   Pray that the anointing of increase and the miraculous will flow into the church.

And through the hands of the apostles many signs and wonders were done among the people. And believers were increasingly added to the Lord, multitudes of both men and women...

—Acts 5:12, 14

45.   Pray that God's Word will be preached with integrity and power in the church.

And my speech and my preaching were not with persuasive words of human wisdom, but in demonstration of the Spirit and of power, that your faith should not be in the wisdom of men but in the power of God.

—1 Corinthians 2:4

46.   Pray for the supernatural harvest of souls.

Then those who gladly received his word were baptized; and that day about three thousand souls were added to them.

And they continued steadfastly in the apostles' doctrine and fellowship, in the breaking of bread, and in prayers.

—Acts 2:41–42

47. Call to the east and west, north and south, commanding souls to come in and know the Lord.

I will say to the north, 'Give them up!' And to the south, 'Do not keep them back!' Bring My sons from afar, and My daughters from the ends of the earth—

—Isaiah 43:6

48. Pray for the stability of the church and overthrow every weapon of satanic attack.

"...No weapon formed against you shall prosper, and every tongue which rises against you in judgment you shall condemn. This is the heritage of the servants of the LORD, and their righteousness is from Me," says the LORD.

—Isaiah 54:17

49. Bind every spirit of Jezebel operating in the church.

For so it was, while Jezebel massacred the prophets of the LORD, that Obadiah had taken one hundred prophets and hidden them, fifty to a cave, and had fed them with bread and water.

—1 Kings 18:4

Nevertheless I have a few things against you, because you allow that woman Jezebel, who calls herself a prophetess, to teach and seduce My servants to commit sexual immorality and eat things sacrificed to idols..

—Revelation 2:20

50. Pray for the congregants that they will honor the Lord through lifestyles of holiness.

I speak in human terms because of the weakness of your flesh. For just as you presented your members as slaves of uncleanness, and of lawlessness leading to more lawlessness, so now present your members as slaves of righteousness for holiness.

—Romans 6:19

51. Pray that the congregants will be responsive to the work of God in the church.

In Him you also trusted, after you heard the word of truth, the gospel of your salvation...Therefore I also, after I heard of your faith in the Lord Jesus and your love for all the saints, do not cease to give thanks for you, making mention of you in my prayers: that the God of our Lord Jesus Christ, the Father of glory, may give to you the spirit of wisdom and revelation in the knowledge of Him...

—Ephesians 1:13, 15–17

52. Overthrow every spirit of confusion, suspicion, division, and strife in the church.

For where envy and self-seeking exist, confusion and every evil thing are there. But the wisdom that is from above is first pure, then peaceable, gentle, willing to yield, full of mercy and good fruits, without partiality and without hypocrisy.

—James 3:16–17

GIVE ME THIS MOUNTAIN

53. Set your goals for the coming months and set them before God.

Now therefore, give me this mountain of which the LORD spoke in that day...It may be that the LORD will be with me, and I shall be able to drive them out as the LORD said.

—Joshua 14:12

Then the king said to me, "What do you request?" So I prayed to the God of heaven. And I said to the king, "If it pleases the king, and if your servant has found favor in your sight, I ask that you send me to Judah, to the city of my fathers' tombs, that I may rebuild it."

—Nehemiah 2:4–5

54. Establish your goals in prayer and pray that God will grant you direction.

55. Plead the blood of Jesus concerning your dreams and aspirations.

56. Pray against any and every satanic agent sent to cut short your dreams and aspirations.

57. Pray that God will dismantle every altar of Baal built against your God-given purpose.

58. Pray that God will send favorable circumstances to help fulfill your dreams and goals.

59. Pray against every satanic order set to question the power of God in your life.

60. Pray for God's mercy and exemption from every generational curse that aborts dreams and purpose.

61. Pray against every surprise of the enemy.

62. Pray for fresh rain, anointing, and inspiration to fulfill your God-given purpose.

PRAY FOR THE NATION AND THOSE IN AUTHORITY

63. Pray and cancel satanic claims on the nation and nullify every curse.

And Hezekiah received the letter from the hand of the messengers, and read it; and Hezekiah went up to the house of the LORD, and spread it before the LORD. Then Hezekiah prayed before the LORD, and said:..."O LORD our God, I pray, save us from his hand, that all the kingdoms of the earth may know that You are the LORD God, You alone".

—2 Kings 19: 14–15, 19

64.	Cancel and nullify every covenant that was enacted with the devil for this nation.

God brings them out of Egypt; He has strength like a wild ox. For there is no sorcery against Jacob, Nor any divination against Israel. It now must be said of Jacob and of Israel, "Oh, what God has done!"

—Numbers 23: 22–23

65.	Decree the peace and protection of America.

66.	Release God's divine intervention and will for America.

67.	Pray for Homeland Security, FBI, CIA, and the U.S. Armed Forces; pray that God will give them the spirit of discernment and a prophetic eye to locate the enemies of freedom and justice and of peace.

68.	Pray that the Lord will expose every form of political corruption in the nation.

Now it came to pass when Samuel was old that he made his sons judges over Israel...But his sons did not walk in his ways; they turned aside after dishonest gain, took bribes, and perverted justice.

—1 Samuel 8:1, 3

69.	Pray that the pursuit of righteousness will increase in the nation.

Righteousness exalts a nation, but sin is a reproach to any people.

70. Nullify every form of spiritual darkness controlling the nation.

Now Satan stood up against Israel, and moved David to number Israel.

—1 Chronicles 21:1

71. Pray that every "Ahithophel" in government will lose favor.

Then someone told David, saying, "Ahithophel is among the conspirators with Absalom." And David said, "O LORD, I pray, turn the counsel of Ahithophel into foolishness!"

—2 Samuel 15:31

72. Pray that God will expose the counsel of wicked men in high places and dethrones them.

73. Pray for the removal of corrupt officials in high places in the nation, seeking to oppress God's people.

Then King Ahasuerus said to Queen Esther and Mordecai the Jew, "Indeed, I have given Esther the house of Haman, and they have hanged him on the gallows because he tried to lay his hand on the Jews.

—Esther 8:7

74. Prophesy against all satanic manipulations in high places.

For we do not wrestle against flesh and blood, but against principalities, against powers, against the rulers of the darkness of this age, against spiritual hosts of wickedness in the heavenly places.

—Ephesians 6:12

75. Pray that all national saboteurs and betrayers will be replaced by men of God's purpose.

So the king took off his signet ring, which he had taken from Haman, and gave it to Mordecai; and Esther appointed Mordecai over the house of Haman.

—Esther 8:2

76.   Pray that God will raise Daniels in the land (Daniel 2:48).

Then the king promoted Daniel and gave him many great gifts; and he made him ruler over the whole province of Babylon, and chief administrator over all the wise men of Babylon.

—Daniel 2:48

77.   Pray that the President and his vice president will be controlled by the hand of God.

It is an abomination for kings to commit wickedness, for a throne is established by righteousness.

—Proverbs 16:12

The king's heart is in the hand of the LORD, like the rivers of water; He turns it wherever He wishes.

—Proverbs 21:1

RESTORATION

78.   Command the recovery of your inheritance.

79.   Raise God's standard to destroy every witchcraft interference and threatening over your life and the lives of your loved ones.

Therefore take up the whole armor of God, that you may be able to withstand in the evil day, and having done all, to stand...above all, taking the shield of faith with which you will be able to quench all the fiery darts of the wicked one.

—Ephesians 6:13, 16

80. Pray that the prophetic pronouncements of God on your life will come to fulfillment.

This charge I commit to you, son Timothy, according to the prophecies previously made concerning you, that by them you may wage the good warfare...

—1 Timothy 1:18

81. Command doors of favor to be opened to you on every side.

82. Pray that everything the enemy has stolen will be restored back to you many-fold.

83. Pray for the spirit of the over taker to possess you that you might overtake the enemy and spoil him in battle.

84. Pray for restoration in any area of your life that the enemy has brought you down.

85. Pray for unrestricted access to favor and success.

86. Pray that God will frustrate every plan of the enemy and confirm His word in your life.

Thus says the LORD, your Redeemer...Who frustrates the signs of the babblers, and drives diviners mad; Who turns wise men backward, and makes their knowledge foolishness; Who confirms the word of His servant, and performs the counsel of His messengers...

—Isaiah 44:1, 25–26

87. Pray to destroy all limitation put upon your life by the enemy and his agents.

88. Pray to reverse and annul all manipulations and satanic schemes caused as a result of past sins.

YEAR OF DIVINE ACCELERATION AND FAVOR

89. Pray to receive the anointing that came upon Elijah and caused him to outrun chariots.

*Then the hand of the LORD came upon Elijah; and he gird-
ed up his loins and ran ahead of Ahab to the entrance of
Jezreel.*

—1 Kings 18:46

90. Declare that you are coming out of the prison of limitation.

*Then Pharaoh sent and called Joseph, and they brought him
quickly out of the dungeon...Then Pharaoh said to
Joseph..."You shall be over my house, and all my people
shall be ruled according to your word...See, I have set you
over all the land of Egypt."*

—Genesis 41:14, 39–42

91. Command a breakthrough that will bless your generation
and future generations.

*He is the LORD our God; His judgments are in all the earth.
He remembers His covenant forever, The word which He
commanded, for a thousand generations...*

—Psalm 105:7–8

92. Decree divine acceleration to the changes you expect in
every sector of life and pray to recover all the property the
enemy has stolen from you.

*So David inquired of the LORD, saying, "Shall I pursue this
troop? Shall I overtake them?" And He answered him,
"Pursue, for you shall surely overtake them and without fail
recover all."*

—1 Samuel 30:8

93. Command confusion into the camp of the enemy.

*Let my accusers be clothed with shame, and let them cover
themselves with their own disgrace as with a mantle.*

—Psalm 109:29

94.   Declare that you will achieve things beyond your dreams and
      hope according to the workings of God's power in you.

      *...work out your own salvation with fear and trembling; for
      it is God who works in you both to will and to do for His
      good pleasure.*
                                                —Philippians 4:12–13

95.   Pray for the kind of breakthrough that cancels the pain of the
      past .

      *You have turned for me my mourning into dancing; You
      have put off my sackcloth and clothed me with gladness...*
                                                —Psalm 30:11

96.   Command accelerated breakthrough of the ploughman
      overtaking the reaper.

      *"Behold, the days are coming", says the LORD, "when the
      plowman shall overtake the reaper, and the treader of
      grapes him who sows seed; the mountains shall drip with
      sweet wine, and all the hills shall flow with it.*
                                                —Amos 9:13

97.   Pray for manifestations of the promises of God concerning
      your life.

Divine Blessings for Pastors and Spiritual Leaders

98.   Command and displace any personality that stands at the
      door to the pastor's blessings, opportunity, favor and break-
      through.

99.   Bind and arrest any surprises of the enemy put in place
      against the pastor's family.

100. Loose the wealth of the nations for prosperity of the gospel
      and the work placed into the pastor's hands for the redemp-
      tion of nations.

101. Loose the mantle of the pastor to operate at his/her maximum potential.

102. Loose the pastor from every agitation, vexation and intimidation.

103. Loose favor, honor, success, and access to all ordained open doors for the pastor.

104. Pray for increase of the spirit of intercession, supplication and grace upon the pastor.

105. Pray for financial stability and increase for the pastor and his/her family to allow them to fulfill their mandate.

BREAKING AND UPROOTING CURSES

106. Declare your freedom from every satanic captivity, bondage and setback.

You area my hiding place; You shall preserve me from trouble; You shall surround me with songs of deliverance.
—Psalm 32:7

107. Take authority over every trap and snare the enemy has planted in your path and decree that they shall fall into their own traps.

Our soul has escaped as a bird from the snare of the fowlers; The snare is broken, and we have escaped. Our help is in the name of the LORD, Who made heaven and earth.
—Psalm 124:7–8

108. Renounce every curse that works in the city or the field against you.

Blessed shall you be in the city and blessed shall you be in the country.
—Deuteronomy 28:3

109. Take authority over every strongman of opposition in your life. Bind and demobilize him and declare your freedom from his stronghold in Jesus' name.

No one can enter a strong man's house and plunder his goods, unless he first binds the strong man. And then he will plunder his house.

—Mark 3:27

110. Disentangle the cords that satan has woven around you.

The LORD is righteous; He has cut in pieces the cords of the wicked. Let all those who hate Zion be put to shame and turned back.

—Psalm 129:4–5

111. Break the hold of all seducing spirits over your life.

Now the Spirit expressly says that in latter times some will depart from the faith, giving heed to deceiving spirits and doctrines of demons, speaking lies in hypocrisy, having their own conscience seared with a hot iron...

—1 Timothy 4:1

DIVINE HEALING

112. Declare that you are healed by the stripes of Jesus.

But He was wounded for our transgressions, He was bruised for our iniquities; The chastisement for our peace was upon Him, and by His stripes we are healed.

—Isaiah 53:5

113. Claim your healing NOW, in Jesus' name.

...who Himself bore our sins in His own body on the tree, that we, having died to sins, might live for righteousness— by whose stripes you were healed..

—1 Peter 2:24

114. Claim deliverance from every affliction in your life.

In all their affliction He was afflicted, and the Angel of His Presence saved them; In His love and in His pity He redeemed them; And He bore them and carried them all the days of old.

—Isaiah 63:9

115. Curse the root of every infirmity and declare that the price for your healing is already paid.

...And He cast out the spirits with a word, and healed all who were sick, that it might be fulfilled which was spoken by Isaiah the prophet, saying: "He Himself took our infirmities and bore our sicknesses."

—Matthew 8:16–17

116. Speak to every visible symptom of disease and sickness and command them to die.

For the law of the Spirit of life in Christ Jesus has made me free from the law of sin and death.

—Romans 8:2

117. Regardless of what you see in the natural, declare that Christ has healed you already.

Now faith is the substance of things hoped for, the evidence of things not seen.

—Hebrews 11:1

118. Pray for grace to walk in obedience and not to provoke the Egyptian curses upon your life.

And the LORD will take away from you all sickness, and will afflict you with none of the terrible diseases of Egypt which you have known, but will lay them on all those who hate you.

—Deuteronomy 7:15

119. Prophesy long life and good health in your life and the lives of your family.

120. Declare your redemption from every curse.

Christ has redeemed us from the curse of the law, having become a curse for us (for it is written, "Cursed is everyone who hangs on a tree")...

—Galatians 3:13

MOVING MOUNTAINS

121. Prophesy against every satanic mountain of confrontation and command it to crumble in Jesus name.

Who are you, O great mountain? Before Zerubbabel you shall become a plain! And he shall bring forth the capstone with shouts of "Grace, grace to it!

—Zechariah 4:7

122. Prophesy confusion into the camp of those plotting your downfall.

Let them be ashamed and brought to mutual confusion who rejoice at my hurt; Let them be clothed with shame and dishonor who exalt themselves against me.

—Psalm 35:26

123. Prophesy that the valley of your battle will be reserved to be the valley of blessing.

Blessed is the man whose strength is in You, whose heart is set on pilgrimage. As they pass through the Valley of Baca, they make it a spring; The rain also covers it with pools. They go from strength to strength; Each one appears before God in Zion.

—Psalm 84:5–7

124. Prophesy and speak to the impossible situation confronting you in your careers and command a change.

"...if you have faith as a mustard seed, you will say to this mountain, 'Move from here to there,' and it will move; and nothing will be impossible for you. However, this kind does not go out except by prayer and fasting."

—Matthew 17:20–21

125. Overthrow the spirit of stagnation and setback confronting your progress in life.

126. Prophesy and decree that affliction will not come into your life the second time.

What do you conspire against the LORD? He will make an utter end of it. Affliction will not rise up a second time.

—Nahum 1:9

127. Prophesy and decree that you shall no longer labor in vain.

Therefore, my beloved brethren, be steadfast, immovable, always abounding in the work of the Lord, knowing that your labor is not in vain in the Lord.

—1 Corinthians 15:58

128. Take authority over and arrest every spirit of robbery operating in your life.

The thief does not come except to steal, and to kill, and to destroy. I have come that they may have life, and that they may have it more abundantly.

—John 10:10

129. Take authority over every prison wall that has caged your life and prophesy and command a turnaround.

The Spirit of the LORD is upon Me, because He has anointed Me to preach the gospel to the poor; He has sent Me to heal the brokenhearted, to proclaim liberty to the captives and recovery of sight to the blind, to set at liberty those who are oppressed; to proclaim the acceptable year of the LORD.

—Luke 4:18–19

DIVINE ELEVATION

130. Ask the Lord that those who may be hindering your promotion will be overthrown.

For promotion cometh neither from the east, nor from the west, nor from the south. But God is the judge: he putteth down one, and setteth up another.

—Psalm 75:6–7 KJV

131. Declare that those who are expecting your harm will be surprised by your promotion.

If it had not been the LORD who was on our side, when men rose up against us, Then they would have swallowed us alive, when their wrath was kindled against us...Blessed be the LORD, Who has not given us as prey to their teeth. Our soul has escaped as a bird from the snare of the fowlers...

—Psalm 124:2–3, 6–7

132. Announce that the day of your promotion is here in Jesus name.

You will arise and have mercy on Zion; For the time to favor her, Yes, the set time has come.

—Psalm 102:13

133. Declare the promotion of the Lord will single you out of the lot.

You love righteousness and hate wickedness; Therefore God, Your God, has anointed You with the oil of gladness more than Your companions.

—Psalm 45:7

134. Decree promotion even in a foreign land in Jesus name.

Then the king promoted Daniel and gave him many great gifts; and he made him ruler over the whole province of Babylon, and chief administrator over all the wise men of Babylon.

—Daniel 2:48

135. Decree a divine favor of elevation in the sight of the enemy.

You prepare a table before me in the presence of my enemies; You anoint my head with oil; My cup runs over.

—Psalm 23:5

136. Declare by faith that irrespective of your educational, financial and physical setback, you will make it in life.

This Book of the Law shall not depart from your mouth, but you shall meditate in it day and night, that you may observe to do according to all that is written in it. For then you will have good success.

—Joshua 1:8

137. Command every cycle of degradation in your life to be broken in Jesus name.

...forgetting those things which are behind and reaching forward to those things which are ahead, I press toward the goal for the prize of the upward call of God in Christ Jesus.

—Philippians 4:13–14

138. Declare that you will manifest the anointing of excellence.

Then this Daniel distinguished himself above the governors and satraps, because an excellent spirit was in him; and the king gave thought to setting him over the whole realm.

—Daniel 6:3

139. Declare that your hand shall be lifted to possess the land (Deuteronomy 30:5).

Then the LORD your God will bring you to the land which your fathers possessed, and you shall possess it. He will prosper you and multiply you more than your fathers.

—Deuteronomy 30:5

STANDING IN THE GAP FOR YOUR CHILDREN

140. Prophesy and declare that your children shall be like olive trees around your homes.

Your wife shall be like a fruitful vine in the very heart of your house, your children like olive plants all around your table. Behold thus shall the man be blessed who fears the LORD.

—Psalm 128:3–4

141. Pray and bind every spirit of rebellion in children and declare that they will walk in obedience.

Children, obey your parents in the Lord, for this is right. "Honor your father and mother," which is the first commandment with promise: "that it may be well with you and you may live long on the earth." And you, fathers, do not provoke your children to wrath, but bring them up in the training and admonition of the Lord.

—Ephesians 6:1–4

142. Overthrow every negative peer pressure in their lives.

He who walks with wise men will be wise, but the companion of fools will be destroyed.

—Proverbs 13:20

143. Release the right support system both at home, in church and at school.

144. Prophesy that your children will have an intimate relationship with God.

All your children shall be taught by the LORD, and great shall be the peace of your children.

—Isaiah 54:13

145. Pray that like Samuel your children will experience God in their youth.

But Samuel ministered before the LORD, even as a child, wearing a linen ephod...And the child Samuel grew in stature, and in favor both with the LORD and men.

—1 Samuel 2:18,26

146. Command the release of their gifting and calling and the call of God over their lives.

Train up a child in the way he should go, and when he is old he will not depart from it.

—Proverbs 22:6

147. Loose the minds of the children from satanic control.

Now the sons of Eli were corrupt; they did not know the LORD.

—1 Samuel 2:12

148. Declare that excellence will be their portion.

Then Daniel was brought in before the king. The king spoke "...I have heard of you, that the Spirit of God is in you, and that light and understanding and excellent wisdom are found in you.

—Daniel 5:13–14

149. Pray that the reverential fear of the Lord will be the most dominant factor in their lives.

Come, you chidren, listen to me; I will teach you the fear of the LORD.

—Psalm 34:11

150. Take authority and dismantle the works of the enemy in their lives.

And have no fellowship with the unfruitful works of darkness, but rather expose them.

—Ephesians 5:11

151. Bind and terminate the power of spirits of accidents, and any spirit assigned to cause any form of pain and affliction.

152. Thank God for the future of children.

For I know the thoughts that I think toward you, says the LORD, thoughts of peace and not of evil, to give you a future and hope.

—Jeremiah 29:11

153. Pray that sick children will be healed completely.

He said to them, "Make room, for the girl is not dead, but sleeping."...When the crowd was put outside, He went in and took her by the hand, and the girl arose.

—Matthew 9:24–25

154. Cancel every assignment of death against the children in Jesus name.

I shall not die, but live, and declare the works of the LORD.

—Psalm 118:17

155. Praise God for your children and dedicate them to the Lord.

Then she made a vow and said "O LORD of hosts, if You will indeed look on the affliction of Your maidservant...but will give your maidservant a male child, then I will give him to the LORD all the days of his life...

—1 Samuel 1:11

156. Pray that the Lord will bless your children with supernatural intelligence.

Then the LORD spoke to Moses, saying: "See, I have called by name Bezalel...And I have filled him with the Spirit of God, in wisdom, in understanding, in knowledge, and in all manner of workmanship...

—Exodus 31:1–3

Breaking Through Impossible Situations

157. Ask the Lord for divine insight for every situation that seems impossible.

But let patience have its perfect work, that you may be perfect and complete, lacking nothing. If any of you lacks wisdom, let him ask of God, who gives to all liberally and without reproach, and it will be given to him.

—James 1:4–5

158. Prophesy advance victory over every battle and situation.

Then the Spirit of the LORD came upon Jahaziel....And he said, "Listen, all you of Judah and you inhabitants of Jerusalem, and you, King Jehoshaphat! Thus says the LORD to you: 'Do not be afraid nor dismayed because of this great multitude, for the battle is not yours, but God's.'"

—2 Chronicles 20:14–15

159. Employ and deploy the cannon balls of God and demolish satanic strongholds standing in your way to victory.

160. Pray and bind every spirit of nightmares and evil dreams.

I will both lie down in peace, and sleep; For You alone, O LORD, make me dwell in safety.

—Psalm 4:8

161. Prophesy and declare that you will leap over the wall that the enemy has erected in your path.

For by you I can run against a troop, By my God I can leap over a wall.

—Psalm 18:29

162. Pray that the Lord will go ahead of you in every venture and make the hidden things plain to you.

You have heard; See all this. And will you not declare it? I have made you hear new things from this time, even hidden things, and you did not know them.

—Isaiah 48:6

163. Command victory over every evil eye and evil tongue operating against you.

No weapon formed against you shall prosper, and every tongue which rises against you in judgment you shall condemn. This is the heritage of the servants of the LORD...

—Isaiah 54:17

164. Prophesy and overthrow every spirit of disgrace, reproach and shame working in our lives.

Do not fear, for you will not be ashamed; Neither be disgraced, for you will not be put to shame; For you will forget the shame of your youth, and will not remember the reproach of your widowhood anymore.

—Isaiah 54:4

DEALING WITH MESSENGERS OF SATAN

165. Pray for public exposure of satanic impressions, projections, and expectations forming in satanic wombs against men and women of God—their lives, and destiny.

166. Invoke the blood of Jesus against satanic retaliations.

167. Decree by the efficacy of the eternal blood of Jesus that there will be a permanent stop to that which has been fighting against your divine mandate and gifting, threatening your future.

168. Pray that the voice of the accuser will be silenced.

169. Pray that those who devise your hurt will be arrested by the Spirit of God, causing their ungodly wisdom to fail.

170. Pray for divine turnaround in marriages, families, finances, and ministries by the superior blood of Jesus.

171. Pray that heaven and earth will testify against the wickedness plotted against the redeemed of the Lord.

...the triumphing of the wicked is short...The heavens will reveal his iniquity, and the earth will rise up against

him...This is the portion from God for a wicked man, the heritage appointed to him by God.

—Job 20: 5,27, 29

172. Pray for the salvation of those enemies who use political power to hurt God's people.

But I say to you, love your enemies, bless those who curse you, do good to those who hate you, and pray for those who spitefully use you and persecute you, that you may be sons of your Father in heaven...

—Matthew 5:44–45

DEALING WITH SATANIC SNARES AND SURPRISES

173. Pray against exploitation, manipulation, sex addictions, drug addictions, and decree divine release by the blood of Jesus.

174. Pray against every unrighteous decree and prediction of misfortune on God's people and your nation.

175. Declare a divine rescue of victims, of children of Zion, from the strong man and his cruelty.

...He sets the poor on high, far from affliction, and makes their families like a flock. The righteous see it and rejoice, and all iniquity stops its mouth.

—Psalm 107: 41–42

176. Pray that those who make cruel and unfair laws that will not favor Zion will be in trouble.

Woe to those who decree unrighteous decrees, who write misfortune, which they have prescribed to rob the needy of justice, and to take what is right from the poor of My people...

—Isaiah 10: 1–2

177. Contend for the prophetic word concerning your life, future, finances, job opportunities, and family. Enforce the total manifestation and fruition of the Word of God over your life.

178. Pray and de-program satanic programs and satanic tactics and calculations against your finances, family, friends, future and destiny.

179. Decree and declare total emancipation from every form of satanic subversion, satanic entanglement and ungodly soul ties. Decree an unconditional release and a total turnaround.

180. Command the restoration of riches and the favor of God for the years the locusts have eaten.

So I will restore to you the years that the swarming locust has eaten, the crawling locust, the consuming locust, and the chewing locust, My great army which I sent among you. You shall eat in plenty and be satisfied, and praise the name of the LORD your God...

—Joel 2:25–26

181. Pray that every ungodly soul tie forged against men and women of God, to confine their mantles, giftings, and callings so that they will not operate at their maximum potential, be broken.

Take Back Your Destiny

182. Pray that the works of the wicked will be confounded, that what they have planted and spoken will whither. Pray for their salvation.

183. Pray and terminate every satanic mockery.

184. Bind every spirit and curse of poverty and annihilate it from your life, finances, and business in the name of Jesus.

185. Decree the reversal of every satanic incantation and invocation from the underworld to undermine your fulfillment of prophecy.

"For there is no sorcery against Jacob, nor any divination against Israel. It now must be said of Jacob and of Israel, 'Oh, what God has done!'"

—Numbers 23:23

186. Cancel every satanic decree against your local church, against the vision and the visionary of this house.

Remove from me reproach and contempt, for I have kept Your testimonies. Princes also sit and speak against me, but Your servant meditates on Your statues. Your testimonies also are my delight and my counselors.

—Psalm 119:22–24

187. Overturn the wicked ideas and calculations in satanic incubators concerning the people of God.

188. Pray against satanic manipulations by the enemy.

189. Command divine acceleration and empowerment for the harvest. Pray for maximum performance and liberty for maximum expression.

190. Abort all time sensitive curses.

191. Decree victory over the Devil through the blood of the Lamb according to Revelation 12:11.

192. By faith, decree a performance of the mind of God concerning you, your church, and the church worldwide. Release honor and glory.

Blessed is she who believed, for there will be a fulfillment of those things which were told her from the Lord.

—Luke 1:45

193. Come against and terminate every spirit of disappointment, nonperformance, underperformance, and setback.

194. Decree that the enemy will be unable to perform their evil devices.

For they intended evil against You; They devised a plot which they are not able to perform.

—Psalm 21:11

GENERAL PRAYER POINTS

195. Destroy blessing blockers, promise blockers, prophecy blockers, expectation blockers, joy blockers, happiness blockers and peace blockers.

196. Break the curses of unavailable love and unavailable blessings.

Christ has redeemed us from the curse of the law, having become a curse for us (for it is written, "Cursed is everyone who hangs on a tree")...

—Galatians 3:13

197. Deal with sickness and disease that are hidden in the vital organs of God's people by the enemy to take their lives prematurely; diseases that are planted by the enemy through food, water, liquid, emotional relationships, and soul ties or past sexual intercourse.

...And He cast out the spirits with a word, and healed all who were sick, that it might be fulfilled which was spoken by Isaiah the prophet, saying: "He Himself took our infirmities and bore our sicknesses."

—Matthew 8:16–17

198. Release and command the manifestation of unfulfilled prophecies, desires, expectations and unfulfilled promises, dreams and visions.

"...Also your people shall all be righteous; They shall inherit the land forever, the branch of My planting, the work of My hands, that I may be glorified. A little one shall become a thousand, and a small one a strong nation. I, the LORD, will hasten it in its time."

—Isaiah 60:22

DEALING WITH PRINCIPALITIES

199. Arrest the ruling principality responsible for all forms of delay in the life of God's people; the principality responsible for financial delays.

Assuredly, I say to you, whatever you bind on earth will be bound in heaven, and whatever you loose on earth will be loosed in heaven.

—Matthew 18:18

200. Deal with every principality responsible for delaying the manifestation of the promises of God to His children.

For we do not wrestle against flesh and blood, but against principalities, against powers, against the rulers of the darkness of this age, against spiritual hosts of wickedness in the heavenly places.

—Ephesians 6:12

201. Deal with the principality responsible for all forms of barrenness and all forms of unfruitfulness in the lives of God's people and the church.

Behold, I give you the authority to trample on serpents and scorpions, and over all the power of the enemy, and nothing shall by any means hurt you.

—Luke 10:19

202. Terminate the enemy's source of life, power, and information; cut all their communication lines; shut off all their radar systems; cut all their links and shut down their evil networks; release confusion into their ranks and files in the name of Jesus.

203. Overthrow the devil's wisdom tables and command their expectations of you and our children to be cut off. Command the opposite of their expectations to occur.

> *On the day that the enemies of the Jews had hoped to overpower them, the opposite occurred, in that the Jews themselves overpowered those who hated them.*
>
> —Esther 9:1

204. Command and the reverse of hidden treasures.

205. Suspend all satanic attacks on the finances and resources of the church and the people of God.

206. Declare that all prisoners of war and spiritual prisoners be acquitted and discharged.

207. Pray for every ministry of your church to be infused with the power of God, to receive anointed direction and empowering to meet the needs of every person in the congregation.

208. Deal with the spirits of Absalom, Judas, Jezebel, Vashti and Delilah that seek to control and subvert the church and its leadership.

TERRITORIAL SPIRITS

209. Deal with territorial spirits in your area assigned to undermine the vision of the church, and the mandate of the pastor and his or her family.

210. Command every knee to bow, of things in heaven, on earth, and under the earth to the name of Jesus Christ, according to Philippians 2:10.

211. Command all things that are in opposition, visible or invisible, to be made subject to the obedience of Christ.

212. Command principalities assigned to hold back the resources of this land to give it back into the hands of God's people.

213. Command the enemy to return your goods and take their hands off you in the name of Jesus.

He swallows down riches and vomits them up again; God casts them out of his belly.

—Job 20:15

214. Command and declare that God will turn your mourning into dancing, your captivity to freedom, so that you can serve Him like you have never served Him before.

He has sent Me to heal the brokenhearted, to proclaim liberty to the captives...to console those who mourn in Zion, to give them beauty for ashes, the oil of joy for mourning, the garment of praise for the spirit of heaviness; that they may be called trees of righteousness, the planting of the LORD, that He may be glorified.

—Isaiah 61:3

215. Pray against spirits that cause delays, which are designed to create provocation, vexation, agitation, and any device created to resist divine change in the life of God's servant, ministry, family, the church and God's people.

Then the LORD answered me and said: "Write the vision and make it plain on tablets, that he may run who reads it. For the vision is yet for an appointed time; but at the end it will speak, and it will not lie. Though it tarries, wait for it; Because it will surely come, it will not tarry.

—Habakkuk 2:2-3

216. Decree an extension of the life span of God's people and the release of everything that should have happened by now that

has not happened. Release money, husbands, children, wives, houses, debt cancellation, scholarships, sponsorships, green cards, promotions, new jobs, salary increases, divine turnarounds, favor, school loan payments, cars and support networks.

"...Bring all the tithes into the storehouse, that there may be food in My house, and try Me now in this," says the LORD of hosts, "If I will not open for you the windows of heaven and pour out for you such blessing that there will not be room enough to receive it."

—Malachi 3:10

PRIORITY OF PRAYER

From this abbreviated practical guide of biblical declarations, you can understand how easy it is to make prayer a priority in your life. The scriptural admonitions to "all kinds of prayer" and "prayer without ceasing" must be obeyed if we are to see the Kingdom of God manifested in the earth. Prayer is God's way. It is written of Moses, the great intercessor, that God "made known His ways to Moses." He learned how to intercede so effectively that God spared a nation His wrath through the prayers of this godly leader.

What will God do in the earth when His Church truly becomes a "house of prayer for all nations"? It is up to each of us to dedicate our lives to the ways of God to see His purposes fulfilled in the earth.

If you come to Jesus as the disciples did, with a simple cry, "Teach us to pray"—He will. And you will be ushered into prayer in another dimension that will transform your life, your family, your church, your community, and your nation.

BIBLIOGRAPHY

Agyin Asare, Charles. *Power in Prayer: Taking Your Blessings by Force.* Hoornaar, The Netherlands: His Printing, 2001.

Ashimolowo, Matthew. *The Power of Positive Prayer. 2000 Prayer Points, 10 Ways to Get Heaven's Attention.* London: Mattyson Media Company, 1996.

Cho, Dr. David Yonggi. *The Fourth Dimension.* Gainesville, FL: Bridge-Logos, 1979.

Cho, Dr. David Yonggi. *Prayer: Key to Revival,* Waco, TX: Word Books, 1984.

Curran, Sue. *Freer Than You Ever Dreamed.* Columbus, GA: TEC Publications, 2005.

Curran, Sue. *I Saw Satan Fall Like Lightning.* Lake Mary, FL: Creation House, 1998.

Curran, Sue. *The Praying Church.* Lake Mary, FL: Creation House, 2004.

Duncan-Williams, Archbishop Nicholas, *Praying Through the Promises of God,* South Bend, IN: Bishop House, 1999. Available at http://www.churchontheweb.com/bookshop/nicholasduncan-williams/index.htm.

Hayes, Norvel. *Pleasing the Lord*. Cleveland, TN: Norvel Hayes Ministries, 1997.

Pickett, Fuchsia. *Understanding the Personality of the Holy Spirit*. Lake Mary, FL: Charisma House, 2004.

Sacks, Cheryl. *The Prayer Saturated Church*. Colorado Springs, CO: Pray! Books, NavPress, 2004.

Additional copies of this book and other book titles from DESTINY IMAGE are available at your local bookstore.

Call toll free: 1-800-722-6774.

Send a request for a catalog to:

Destiny Image® Publishers, Inc.

P.O. Box 310
Shippensburg, PA 17257-0310

"Speaking to the Purposes of God for this Generation and for the Generations to Come."

For a complete list of our titles, visit us at www.destinyimage.com